LYNN RUTH MILLER

GETTING THE LAST LAUGH

THE INSPIRATIONAL TRUE STORY OF
THE WORLD'S OLDEST PERFORMING COMEDIENNE

EXCENTRIX PRESS

TITLE:

Getting the Last Laugh: The Inspirational True Story of the World's Oldest Performing Comedienne

By Lynn Ruth Miller

First published by excentrix press in 2020

Edited by David Smitherman & Peter Dunbar

Front cover by: Zak Milofsky

Graphic Design: Antonio Morilla

All images are from the author's personal collection.

Contents

Prologue: How I Found Comedy   5

On the World Stage   15

How It All Began   44

California Dreaming   87

The Attack   112

Transitioning   124

Laughing at Seventy   151

Ageing Is Amazing   163

Overcoming Fear   199

Funny Business   215

The Joke's On Me   238

The Best Accident   268

Epilogue: None of This Should Have Happened   285

These are events as I remember them. I feel certain some of the details have been unintentionally clouded by time. Any inaccuracies are a fault of my memory, but the spirit of what I have said remains.

PROLOGUE
How I Found Comedy

I was a failure. I was seventy years old and had done a lot of things well enough, but I never made it big. People would tell me I was great, but when it came to getting the better job or the bigger prize, I was always an also-ran. I *knew* that my big moment would come eventually, but at my age, it was getting late in the game and nothing spectacular was on my horizon. I had managed to earn a master's degree in Journalism from Stanford University way back in 1964 and because I graduated top of the class, I knew I was destined to be a top writer for *The New York Times* or *The Washington Post*. However, destiny did not agree with me. Years and years of submitting, pushing, and hustling managed to land me a few feature articles in small magazines. That is all. Even when I did a series of magazine-length stories in *The Toledo Blade*, I still could not get on the regular staff.

And then I saw it. I was trolling the net for jokes, when I saw an ad for The San Francisco Comedy College and I thought, "This is it! No one can teach someone to be funny; it cannot be done. This place is a rip-off, and I am going to expose it to the world."

I had seen many stories written by reporters who had tried to live on the tiny pittance welfare gives to the starving. Their personal stories broke everyone's heart. They went national, and those writers became famous. Like I wanted to be. Like I was so sure I would be.

If I took that class and told the world to beware of those comedy charlatans, I would finally, after forty years of fruitless effort, make the big time. I called the number listed and left a message explaining that I was a freelance writer for two magazines and a newspaper and would like to take this class to write a story about it. A half-hour later I got a return call. It was Kurtis Matthews, the man who had founded the college four years ago. "I just got your message," he said. "And I love small Jewish women."

At last! Destiny came through! I am about five feet tall and so Semitic looking people daven when they see me. I spew guilt like a rose spreading its fragrance. I am definitely Jewish. When I walk into a bakery, they just hand me bagels. I never have to ask.

"You have arrived," I said to Kurtis, and I enrolled in his class. It was quite an event for me. I rarely had any place to go at night those days. I was, after all, seventy years old, and I did not have a partner or children. I had no family left. I lived alone and spent my days walking dogs, writing articles and painting pictures no one wanted to buy. Suddenly, thanks to Kurtis Matthews and his class, I had a great place to go where I could dress in something a bit more presentable than my sweats and have an experience that was brand-new.

As soon as I walked into the class, he recognized me. "Is this the place where you transform a bunch of clunks into funny people?" I asked.

He nodded. "But you are already funny. The only thing I can teach you is how to hold a microphone and what a routine is. You will do the rest."

"Don't be so sure," I said.

Why should I believe him? I had no idea what standup comedy was. I certainly didn't think of it as a profession or a way to earn a living.

I looked around at the rest of the class, and I have to say they were all adorable. They ranged from 18 to 23 and each one had a special something that brought out the mother in me. Actually, I should say grandmother, since I was about fifty years older than most of them.

The class lasted eight weeks, and I loved being in it. I went to each class and listened to the students talk about their problems and try to make jokes about their lives. I learned the structure of a joke, the rule of three, building the laugh thus: *I shop online all the time… that is how I get (1) vitamins, (2) underwear, (3) and sex.* I learned about call-backs and displacement. *I want a man's man who always gets what he wants. And I found one. . . in prison.*

But the best part of the class was that I had a wonderful time. Kurtis was (and still is) delightful, and I respected the way he encouraged these young people who were so riddled with doubts and insecurities. Yet, even with all his encouragement, I didn't hear any of the students say anything I would call a joke. He explained that the formula for every joke is a set-up (the premise) and punch (the surprise).

Set-up: *I got a lot from my mother.*

Punch: *That's why I have been in therapy for 80 years.*

He had us finish sentences to get the idea. He said, "I ran out …." you finish thus: "of my lover's house and bumped into my wife."

Once you get that structure mastered, you can elaborate and turn your one-liners into stories. But first you have to master the one-liners. Here's one of mine: *They gave me five minutes up here because they think that's all the time I have left.*

After class, a few of us would have coffee together and talk about what we had just tried to learn and what each of us planned to do after the course was over. I was suddenly in a social group that was fun and interesting and far more stimulating than being with my dogs.

One of the students had just discovered that his mother and father both were gay. "They couldn't have always been gay," I said. "They had you, didn't they?"

"Well, he said, "That is what they tell me… but I look an awful lot like my Uncle Jim."

When the talk drifted to dating, I was totally lost. Evidently, things had changed radically from when I was a young, innocent, holding hands with my first boyfriend. The rule in the 1940s was that if your date hadn't kissed you (mouth closed) by the third date, the relationship was going nowhere. Now, according to my new social circle, if you didn't give them a blowjob on the first date, there was no future for the two of you. I, for one, wasn't sure what they meant. I thought a blowjob was what you did to balloons at a children's party. And what was all this talk about back doors? A back door is the entrance to the kitchen.

The class was very loving, forgiving, and lots of fun. The biggest thing I learned was that although sex was freer and the conversational taboos that guided me when I was young no longer existed, people still had the same yearning to be accepted and loved, and they all felt confused about how to make that happen.

Kurtis had a magic about him that inspired us all. Everyone in that first group signed up for the second eight weeks to get even better at comedy and more comfortable on stage. When we completed sixteen weeks, we were eligible to take the final exam, which was a performance at Cobb's Comedy Club in San Francisco. I had taken a lot of final exams, and I was actually pretty good at them, so even though I was only writing an article about the class, I decided to do the performance anyway. I had no intention of doing standup comedy on a stage. For one thing, I had no idea where those stages were.

The only people I saw on stage were actors in a play or a lot of people playing instruments at Davies Symphony Hall.

We were all very nervous about our performance. Kurtis told us that we each were to perform for five minutes. That doesn't sound like a long time, but believe me, when you have never performed on stage before, five minutes feels like five years. I thought about my myriad of experiences and tried to think of what I could talk about for five minutes that would be funny to a young crowd.

The transition from margarine to butter would mean nothing to them. They would not care about my fear of needing dentures. They cared not a whit that we used to choose whether to pump our own gasoline. And then I remembered the horrors of the mammogram. I had managed to endure three of them before I decided, "The hell with this. I am not going to run my body parts through a mangle anymore." And that was the topic I decided to address for my five minutes of fame.

The other six in the class were terrified because they had never spoken in front of a crowd of strangers before. I had been a college professor for six years and speaking to strangers was not what scared me. What worried me was how I could manage to make people less than half my age laugh with me, not at me.

We each walked on stage and managed to remember to hold the mike in front of our faces and move the mike stand so people could see us. The others in the class did their five minutes to unbearable silence. And then it was my turn. It is not easy to approach a nonresponsive audience, but I had no choice. No one else was funny. So, heart beating violently in my chest, hands shaking and mouth dry as sand, this is what I said:

The mammogram is like putting your most vulnerable body part through a mangle...without heat. It was invented by a male surgeon who decided to get back at his mother because she made him finish medical school instead of letting him smoke bongs with the boys. If you women want to prepare for one of these exams, lie down in the garage and have your partner back the car over you. I am all too familiar with this procedure. I go to a place called The Breast Center in San Mateo. Every year, they send me what looks like an embossed party invitation with a phone number on it. I open up the envelope and I think, OMG! It's that time again?

I call the number to make the dreaded appointment. Surprise! No matter what time I request, they always have room for me.

"Monday at midnight? Of course. We are here for you and your breast."

"How nice of you," I say. "How will I find you?"

"Oh, you can see the building from the freeway. It has two huge domes on it. "

Well, I found it and I was thrilled. The place had 24 floors devoted to my breasts. My two husbands couldn't even find them.

I walked into the reception area and an androgynous person handed me a schmatta I wouldn't use to swab my ex-husband's toilet. Mine had prints of dancing ballerinas to remind me that my days of tour jeté were long gone. I was ushered into a beautiful room that looked as if Martha Stewart decorated it… before she went to prison. The walls were filled with lush Renoirs and Laurencin prints. The couches were upholstered with plush velvets in shades of lavender, purple and pink. The lights were low, thank God, so you couldn't see what has happened to your skin.

I took off my bra and put on the blouse, which was open at the front, no fasteners. I joined several other identically clad women with their business hanging out reading, knitting and exchanging high-protein recipes as casually as if we were having tea at The Hilton.

One woman said, "My daughter is in environmental studies. She majored in global warming."

Another fanned herself. "Well, I hope she finds the answer soon. It is boiling in here."

"No, no, honey," I said, "That is a hot flash."

Just then, an immense woman emerged from a door I hadn't noticed. She looked like she'd just finished breastfeeding a dozen babies, not to mention the twenty-six she wet-nursed. She beckoned me into a room that was approximately the temperature of Juneau, Alaska... in a cold snap. My nose dripped and my breath formed white cumulus clouds.

"Take off your blouse," she said.

"I have."

"Then face front," she said.

"I am."

And the two of us spent the next half hour searching for my little treasure, which she insisted I was hiding under my armpit or in my shoe. At last, we found my body part shriveled to the size of a pinhead with frost dripping from the tip. She pointed to a machine that resembled a medieval thumbscrew without the teeth.

"Put it there," she said.

Well, I don't know about you, but I can't just sling it over there. I have to go with it. The tray was obviously designed for Scandinavian women, and I am under five feet tall. After much effort that felt like I was failing an audition for a ballet class, I managed to get my breast on the ice-cold tray. Suddenly, without any warning, thirty-five pounds of steel came crashing down on my breast.

"BREATHE!" she shouted. She approached me, waving my chart in her hand. "That wasn't so bad, was it? Now let's try to find the other one."

"You can't have that one," I said. "It belongs to my boyfriend, and he doesn't like it ironed."

This year, I had a much better experience. I was greeted by a tiny Asian woman who knew right where to look for what she needed. There they were: thin as microfilm, resting peacefully on my navel.

She scanned the X-rays. "You sure are dense," she said.

"No, not me," I told her. "I went to Stanford."

The crowd went wild. They clapped, they cheered, and they laughed and laughed and laughed. I smiled and left the stage unbelievably relieved that my time was over. After the show, we mingled with the audience to thank them for coming and to find out what they thought of the performances. A young man came up to me and asked me to sign his ticket. He smiled at me as if I was the most beautiful human being he had ever seen. I thought to myself, "Oh my God! This kid loves me. And I didn't have to cook him dinner. I didn't have to change the sheets. I am going to do this again." And I did. Again, and again, and again.

I had found my calling.

CHAPTER 1
On the World Stage

I never dreamed that my glorious moment on stage would lead to my traveling all over the world telling jokes to strangers in strange lands. Although I began my brand new comedy career in San Francisco, over the past 16 years I have taken it to England, Scotland, Wales, Australia, Southeast Asia and much of Europe. Here is a smattering of what one of my overseas tours looks like. Just think!! It all began because I wanted to write a story about a comedy college and now at 86 I have one new adventure after another.

Of course these trips didn't just happen. Each one takes months of planning and very often there are slipups along the way. The pace is very demanding, but I always tell myself that since I contracted to do standup comedy, this is what I must do to pursue my career. I am going to tell you about just one of tours and how I deal with things like jet lag when I return home. This is what my life is now. Remember, it took sixteen years to create this kind of a schedule.

I have to admit that I really like all this globetrotting. The planning, the packing, the flights, and accommodations, the endless e-mails and months of pre-planning, are well worth it.

I travel alone, and that means I must arrange for people to meet me in these exotic countries where I do not speak the language, and I must be sure of my accommodations and transport to the shows I am doing. Thank goodness for the internet. All this would be impossible without it. But the internet alone is not enough. I have also discovered a few key people who help me get all this arranged properly so I do not end up stranded in the middle of an ocean.

Dan Dockery from Hanoi is indispensable in making sure I create a manageable itinerary, and Umar Rana in Singapore has figuratively adopted me, making sure people give me a sensible deal. It was he who saved me from financial ruin in Hong Kong. I accepted a gig where I would get 30% of the take with no transportation or hotel provided. It is customary for these two items to be included in your fee when you perform in Asia, but I was so excited about Hong Kong that I didn't think things through. I wrote Umar to ask if he knew an affordable place to stay in Hong Kong. When he heard the arrangement I had made, he told me I must cancel that trip because I would never make enough money to pay for a cab to the hotel, let alone the hotel room.

I apologized to the booker and told him I had to back out because I could not afford the extra costs but, although I didn't know it, Umar wrote him as well and told him why I was cancelling. He added, "You know, this isn't some twenty-year-old backpacker you booked," implying that when someone books a person my age to do a show, they should be a bit more considerate.

I have to say I found his remark funny at first, but when I thought about it, I realized that this is the very thing I always fight. I do not want special consideration because of my age.

Yet, the truth is that I do need that special help because I am well into my eighties. My hearing is horrid and my flexibility, while amazing *for someone my age*, is not what it used to be. This is always my dilemma: I do not ever ask for favors, but in my heart, I know I need them. My mantra has always been that I want the quality of my act to be judged by the same criteria as everyone in the business, but the truth is that people either reject me because they do not believe an old woman can be funny or they think I am far better than I really am because I am so old. It is my catch-22.

I start my tours in a different place each time, but my last one began in Singapore. The flight there is very long: about 17 hours. I could have paid twice as much and gotten there two hours earlier, but I am Jewish. I do not waste money.

I have been thinking about why comedians travel as far as we all do to stand in front of a lot of strangers for as little as ten minutes or as long as an hour talking about ourselves. I can only speak for myself, of course, and for me, living alone as I do, it is worth the travel and the personal inconvenience to have those few moments when I am in the spotlight making a lot of people love me… because in that moment, they do.

But I think it is more than that. We are social animals after all, and interaction feeds our souls. As I get older (and I sure hope I keep doing it), I realize that the impetus to keep doing this is far more than those moments on stage. It is that amazing connection with different people from different backgrounds and the jolt of surprise when I realize how similar our values are and how alike our mutual vision is of what makes "the good life."

I now have a fan base in Singapore, which is very gratifying. Although I am a foreigner invading their comedy scene, they treat me like I have always belonged there. At least three comedians make the effort to come hear me whenever I appear. This is unheard of both in San Francisco and in London. It is rare as hen's teeth for a fellow comedian to make a special effort to see your show. We are all too competitive. I think that is sad. I have always tried to support other comedians because I know all too well how rough and tumble the path to acceptance can be. But very few of my fellow performers make that effort.

The staff at Hero's Bar, where the Singapore show is held, not only knows me but remembers what I like to drink before a show (water) and after (alcohol…a lot of alcohol). On my last trip, Naomi from Jakarta invited the Jewish population of Singapore (which is far larger than I thought) to come to the show, so thirty of the people there were thanks to her.

Umar runs a truly professional show with a top-notch selection of local and international comedians. This time, there was a man from India, Azeem Banatwala, who was truly amazing. He is on TV; very famous in that part of the world. In this show, all the comedians got the laughs they needed to feed their egos and get the crowd going. The Singapore audiences want to laugh and want to support us. They make us all feel like stars.

Usually comedians at my level (in the middle) perform at sleazy pubs with makeshift stages. Hero's is a legitimate club with lovely food and table settings. The audiences Umar attracts are mostly from Singapore. When I go overseas, I usually expect to do comedy for expats: people whose first language is English. In Singapore, most of my audience have English as a second language. As a result, the double entendre and word play do not work.

When I do comedy, I like to address some jokes directly to people in the audience. I usually make a few cracks about Jewish men (inadequate) and Jewish mothers (materialistic tyrants). I look directly at someone sitting near the stage and say something like, "Did *your* mother say that?" At Hero's Bar with more diverse audiences, I got understanding nods. This all goes to prove that people the world over share many hang-ups.

Another thing that makes the comedy in Singapore special is that Umar employs local comedians. Usually when I do an English-speaking show in Asia, most of the lineup is also from English-speaking countries, but not so in Singapore.

After that show, we all stayed to have a drink and get to know one another. This is in contrast to the London experience where the headliner usually comes in just before it is time to do his set (and it is almost always a he) and the rest of the comedians leave the show when they are done performing. The truth is we all should be working together to create a good experience for the audience and to support one another. Each of us brings our own special take on life to the stage. No one person is better than another because each performer presents a unique viewpoint. That is what makes standup comedy so satisfying to the audience. They get a glimpse of another perspective of the life we all are trying to live.

The reason I love these travels is that I get to know the people who perform and those who book me. Most of them have become close friends. I stay with Umar, his wife Sylvie, and their cat Tangerine when I am in Singapore, and they make me feel like part of their family. Sylvie always makes me Czech chicken soup, which isn't like the schmaltzy Jewish tonic my mother made, but much healthier, fat-free, and delicious.

I always hate to leave Singapore because it is such a happy place. The people who live there love it because it is clean and safe, and the standard of living is uniformly comfortable and secure. The air smells fresh. It is as safe as a baby's bedroom to wander through the streets. Their government is a benevolent dictatorship, not a democracy. All the bickering, competition, and hatred that typifies Western democracies are gone. Some of their laws are really unusual, like not being allowed to feed pigeons or buy chewing gum; and that they have public flogging (it's true) but, on the other hand, there is a clarity to the way you can live your life when one man decides what is right and wrong. The amazing thing to me is that in Singapore, evidently, everyone obeys him without argument.

The cost of living is outrageously high there, but so are the salaries. The social care is humane and all-encompassing.

People get food and housing benefits; medical care is organized so that the rich pay for it and the poor get it for little or nothing. People feel safe in that country. This is in sharp contrast to places like the United States where medical care is so expensive, and London, where housing costs are so out of proportion to salaries earned that many people with good jobs are homeless.

The day after that Singapore show, I had a relatively early flight to Ho Chi Minh City. The lovely Sylvie took me to the airport where we shared a cup of coffee and ruminated on what makes life worthwhile. Sylvie is Eastern European and our backgrounds could not be more dissimilar, yet we agree on what makes the good life. Sylvie is much braver than I, however. She is not afraid to leave a situation that is uncomfortable for her. She was in a relationship for several years and one day she woke up and said, "This will never get any better." She walked out and found herself a new job in a new place. Just like that. No long arguments; no agonizing about right or wrong or hurt feelings.

The Singapore Airport is the easiest to navigate of any I have ever been in—spacious, clean, and un-crowded. I managed to find the gate, go through security, and get on the plane with no problem. This sounds fairly simple, but I assure you in a country where you don't know the language and you are not sure of the rules, it is a victory to be able to navigate your arrival with such ease.

I was flying Viet Jet Airlines from Singapore to Ho Chi Minh City. I boarded the plane and we all waited patiently for takeoff. We waited and waited and waited. Finally, there was a blurred announcement, and everyone got up, gathered their belongings, and left the airplane. Evidently, a bird got caught in the propellers and messed up the motor. I didn't know whom to feel sorry for, the bird, the crew, or the discombobulated passengers.

We all trooped back into the airport to another gate, boarded another plane, and waited even longer for takeoff. Coincidentally, I was in the midst of reading a very long book, *The Goldfinch* by Donna Tartt, and was so absorbed in the intricate plot I didn't notice the time evaporating. We were supposed to arrive in Ho Chi Minh City at 2:05 p.m. and we got there at 5:00 p.m. My show began at 8:00 p.m.

Before you can enter Vietnam, you need to buy a visitor's visa for $25. I had the proper forms ready, a photo that made me look like a convicted felon, and the money. I decided I'd better call Quynh, the woman who was supposed to meet me at the airport, because obviously I was not there when she thought I would be. However, I could not get my phone to go online. Although the airport has free wi-fi, the process to access it is written in Vietnamese, so I could not figure it out. Adam, the young man sitting next to me in the waiting room, offered to use his phone to try to contact Quynh but she did not answer his call. He was a pre-med student from India, studying in Singapore, on his way home for a visit. His real name was unpronounceable for me, so he said, "Call me Adam," and that was what I did as he guided me through the exit process. I kept asking him questions but after a few odd responses, I realized that I was talking to two Adams, not one. I would ask one of them a question and expect the other one to answer.

At first, I thought my eyes (which have held up very well so far) were giving up on me. However, Adam assured me I was not seeing double. He had an identical twin whom I also called Adam. The two of them kept trying to call Quynh and when that didn't work, I managed to contact Nick, the man who had booked me for the show. He was living in London and thankfully picked up his phone. He also could not reach Quynh, so the two Adams insisted they would take me to my hotel on the way to theirs.

The trip to the hotel was amazing. There were hundreds of cars and thousands of motorbikes clogging the streets. People were getting ready for the New Year, and they were transporting peach trees and orange trees on their tiny bikes (and not wearing helmets) to decorate in their homes, much as we do Christmas trees. Compared to Singapore, which is spacious, modern, and richly beautiful, the streets in HCMC are narrow and the buildings retain the flavor of the pre-war city. The city has preserved some of its original character and yet it is filled with bright lights and glittering signs that give it a Las Vegas feel. The heat is intense and the air so thick you can practically cut it with a knife. My hotel was clean and bright and very comfortable. At least, I think it was. I didn't have time to look too closely. I had only thirty minutes to unpack and dress for the show.

I finally met Quynh, because Nick had told her to pick me up at the hotel. She was a delight. She is a jack-of-all-trades at the venue, taking tickets, hosting the comedians, and making the patrons feel at home. I featured for JoJo , an established comedian who has been doing this kind of thing for over twenty-five years. It is always an honor for me to be on the bill with women who have broken down the very barriers I face. The audience was very responsive, but the interesting thing was that I thought the evening was a huge success, but JoJo was not happy. The audience was smaller than she expected, and the ambience of the room was not what she had hoped. I realized then how low my expectations were, because I thought it was a gem of an evening. Maybe that isn't a bad thing, because I came away elated with the show, and poor JoJo was miserable.

After the gig, Quynh put me on the back of her bike and off we went to my hotel. We stopped on the way for a bit of Kahlua to finish off the evening…and me. I staggered up to my room, (probably singing a bit louder than I should have) at 2:00 a.m. after Quynh and I made arrangements to spend a few days at her place when I return. She is an artist and so am I. We decided I would do some art and get to see a bit of the countryside on the next trip.

JoJo and I were on the same plane to Hanoi the next morning. Quynh had picked me up and taken me to the airport. She is a very clever woman and managed to get me priority booking for the plane, so I swept through the line to the gate. After a thirty-minute wait, we had to change gates and the flight was delayed. I was getting used to this routine. After all, Viet Jet did the same thing on the trip to HCMC, but this time there wasn't a bird involved. When we finally got to Hanoi, Dan Dockery picked us up like the reliable rock that he is. He located us wandering through the crowd of people and got us back to the very lavish Intercontinental Hotel that sponsors his events.

This hotel room was so luxurious that the bathroom was bigger than my entire one-bedroom London flat. There were so many esoteric features that I needed someone to show me how to turn on the lights. I am from the days where you contacted a person if you needed something. Nowadays, you push a button. Sadly, in my case I can never find the right button. It is the story of my life.

JoJo was very stressed and not feeling well. She had a terrible time trying to get her luggage on the plane, and this, coupled with some indigestion and disappointment over the gig in Ho Chi Minh City, had exhausted her. She went up to her room, which was the size of a three-story mansion, while I toddled over to one of the several cafes in the hotel, each one fit to serve tea to Queen Elizabeth herself. I had one of a series of Caesar salads (the one thing I can count on not to send me vomiting in the ladies' room. This happens far too often when I am in strange countries where they believe fried ant eggs are yummy, dogs are for digesting instead of petting and a coffee costs more than booking a round-the-world cruise.)

I returned to my room, which was so spacious I was amazed I managed to find the bed without a divining rod and napped until show time. While I slumbered, poor JoJo's digestive problems accelerated and, like the understudies in West End shows, she gave me my big moment. She stayed in bed to recuperate and I became the headliner. This was an unexpected bonanza for me. I rarely get to headline, because no one believes I can sustain laughter for over thirty minutes.

I love the room Dan uses for his shows, and his audiences *want* to laugh, so I knew this was going to be the frosting on the cake for me. I did fifty minutes of comedy and every joke worked. I was walking on air when I left the stage, and after I drank the bottle of wine one of the audience members bought for me, I was floating on a cloud so high my feet didn't touch the ground.

Me performing that evening in Hanoi. The stage is set up like a living room so the other comedians are sitting on the couch while you perform. It is an acid test to have your severest critics so close you can hear their silence when you tell a joke.

I think this is what keeps me in this business. The thrill of a successful gig has not worn off for me. It is never just another night. I vaguely remember when I lost my virginity on plastic sheets in a grim motel in Indiana, and I have to say that supposedly cosmic moment did not compare to standing on stage in Hanoi talking dirty to a bunch of expats in a hot little room overlooking the river. That's my kind of magic.

The next morning, Dan's driver took me to the airport, and he told me how life in Hanoi has changed since the war. He said the entire place has been rebuilt and now there are more motorbikes than there are people on the roads. There is also a huge gap between rich and poor. Even more than Ho Chi Minh City, Hanoi has retained its rustic flavor and is always sparkling with colorful lights. The Vietnamese are artistic, creative people who love color and light. The thing I do not understand is how they manage to breathe the fetid air. But they do, and it doesn't seem to affect their disposition. Everyone I met in Vietnam, without exception, was happy and interesting.

My next stop was Bangkok. This was my second time there, the first gig was the one that started this whole series of travel, and it was all because of one man.

I have been going to Ireland twice a year for at least five years. When I plan a trip there, I always send out a mass e-mail to my Irish friends to let them know I will be in town. It had to be two years ago when I sent out one of these announcements and got a return message from my darling buddy Aidan Killian that said, "I am in Bangkok."

I responded," What are you doing there?"

And he answered, "Comedy."

I said, "I would love to do comedy there."

And that is how it all began. Aidan put me in touch with Matthew Wharf, who booked me, and once I got that date in the diary, I added a few more gigs there and continued on to Vietnam and Cambodia. One of those gigs was a small room run by Delfin Solomon. We got along really well, and he immediately asked me to return to Bangkok. We booked this second show almost immediately, and I fashioned the entire tour around it.

Delfin is a professor who teaches film and scriptwriting at the university there. He puts on small, beautiful comedy shows. He arranged for my room with his sponsor, Hotel Galleria 10 Sukhumvit, a place almost as luxurious as Dan's Intercontinental but not nearly as expensive. I had two other shows to do in Bangkok and had to stay two extra nights besides the one that was part of Delfin's hiring package. He also promised to meet me at the airport but did not give me a specific meeting point. The Bangkok Airport looks like Times Square at rush hour. Unless you know where to meet someone, it is almost impossible to find anyone. I knew there would be trouble, and there was.

Delfin assured me he would locate me, but when I got off the plane, he was nowhere in sight. I learned later that he was late because he got caught in the traffic that is always unbelievable in Bangkok. At every hour of the day or night, the streets look more like parking lots than roads. I tried to call him on my phone but could not reach him. I did not know how I would manage to get to my hotel since I had no Thai money. I went to the information desk in the airport and the man on duty there called Delfin for me, but again no answer. Then, I went to the tourist board to see how I could manage to get a taxi and pay for it. While I was trying to figure out how to get where I needed to be, a man standing at the counter (also to get some help), asked me if I would like to use his phone. I asked if he would call Delfin. He tried but there was still no answer.

By this time, I was feeling a bit shaky since I had left the hotel in Hanoi without any breakfast. It was now well after 3:00 p.m. This very kind man said he would take me to my hotel and offered to buy me a coffee and a croissant if I waited for him to buy his tickets to Hong Kong. Meanwhile, I sent Delfin a message that I was in the Starbucks upstairs.

In moments, a woman sat down next to me and introduced herself. She was Kordelia, an aesthetician (they make people young and beautiful for a substantial fee) and the man who helped me was Liam, from Ireland. They both live in Spain in a place called Mojacar Playa. Kordelia's specialty is filling in facial wrinkles, but she wanted to expand her expertise to doing bum lifts. She was in Bangkok to get her certification.

All I could think of was if this woman sees my sagging bottom, she will be so appalled that she will abandon me.

Instead, she and Liam adopted me like their long-lost granny. They drove me to my hotel, a trip that took two hours because of that traffic. On the way, we got to know and like one another. I asked if the two of them would come to the show I was doing that night, and they said they would try.

Galleria 10 is a luxury hotel with a heart. The entire staff worked together to get me up to my room and try to figure out which button turned on the light and which one worked the air conditioning, accustomed as I am to places where I am lucky if the toilet flushes and the lights come on. They helped me get on the internet and left me to try to gather my wits.

Not ten minutes after I got settled in that delightful hotel, Delfin sent me a message asking if I was still in Starbucks. I explained I had been adopted and all was well. Again, I had 30 minutes to change into something presentable to do my first gig in Bangkok. It was a last-minute one because the booker, Chris Wagoda, had heard about me and knew I would be in town. I cannot tell you how exciting that is for someone who lived most of her eighty-some years submerged in a thick cloud of anonymity, composing books no one reads and creating art no one sees; walking dogs, picking up their droppings, and ushering for theatre and musical events dressed in black. No one anywhere knew my name in the United States. In Pacifica, I was the dog lady. At the San Francisco Opera, I was the one who took them to their seats. Isn't it amazing how popular you become if you can tell a good joke?

Chris runs Comedy Club Bangkok, the most successful English-speaking comedy club in the city. I was to headline there, and I really hoped my new fairy godparents, Liam and Kordelia, would come along. Chris, who is unbelievably reliable, sent a man named Sheldon—a swimmer, former surfer, and LA guy—to pick me up, and off we went to do comedy. First, I had to have a meal since all I had eaten in the last 24 hours was that croissant and cup of coffee Liam had bought for me. While I was eating the one thing I trust in Asia (Caesar salad, remember?), in walked Liam and Kordelia. I was thrilled and prayed that the show would be worth their time. Chris, being the gentleman that he is, gave them complimentary tickets and paid for my meal. His show was fast-paced, and the audience loved it. Two girls sitting in the front row were American and once I saw their reaction to the other comedians, I knew I would be okay. They would get the jokes.

One thing I always do is check out my audience before I go on stage. I never walk into a show just in time for my set. I come early to see how conservative the audience is, what the average age is, and what amuses them.

There were about forty-five people attending the show and all of them were comedy ready. I did my headlining set, and it went well. After the show, we went down to the bar. Liam treated me to a couple glasses of wine and told me I must come to Mojacar Playa to do a show. I said I would. They said everyone there loves funny old ladies. I said I hope so. And they took me home to be sure I was safe. And I was.

I used the next morning to catch up on e-mails I had not touched for too many days and then my special buddy Jonathan sent a native Thai gentleman to take me to his club in another neighborhood of the city. Jonathan does comedy in a youth hostel and keeps the prices low, which I support. It reminds me of Angel Comedy in London where the prices are nearly non-existent so that young people can afford a fun night out. I met Jon last year, and we told Jewish jokes all night long. After our show that night, Jon had purchased a pan, a hot plate, and a lot of ingredients so I could create my signature dish: blintzes (Jewish crepes). Six members of the audience stayed after to help with the mixing, beating, and frying, and by God, we made blintzes so authentic that Moses descended for a taste.

The next day I met Matthew Wharf for lunch. Matthew was the man who booked me for my first Bangkok gig a year ago. I got a standing ovation at that show. When I think about it, I am not absolutely sure it WAS a standing ovation. I think the audience stood up because I am so short that they couldn't see me on stage. But once they got to their feet, I called it a standing ovation and posted it all over Facebook. A girl's got to do what a girl's got to do, right?

The next night, Delfin picked me up to go to his club on the outskirts of the city called Comedy Den Pakkret. He had sold thirty tickets, but only fifteen people showed up. The room was in a small park with a Tex-Mex restaurant called Que Pasa. The food was magnificent, and the portions were Texas sized. That means a small salad would feed an Army battalion and you would still have leftovers. I had — you guessed it — a Caesar salad. It was exceptional and big enough to serve to our entire audience…with leftovers.

The line-up for this show was excellent. Tristan, one of the comedians, married an Israeli woman. He was telling me how modern and exciting Tel Aviv has become. He also talked a great deal about how biased the press is against Israel, partly because of Netanyahu's belligerent policies and partly because so much of the press is anti-Zionist. It was a revealing discussion because even though I personally do not like Israel's practices toward the people in Gaza, I never realized there were so many extenuating circumstances. The one observation I made to justify what goes on there is that after the Holocaust, the Jewish people never want to be in a situation where they are not the majority. One can hardly blame them for that.

The next day, I met Aidan Killian , the man who is responsible for all this wonderful travel, and his friend Trevor, another comedian, for lunch. We all agreed stand-up comedy is the last place left where you can say what you really think without fear of being banned. Yet, I have to say that is not as true as it once was. I still hold to the theory that any topic works if you can make it funny. The whole idea is to make people laugh. But sometimes and all too often these days, someone will take offense.

Then it was home to London to freeze after sweating buckets in Bangkok. I had no time to complain or even notice what was happening to my abused metabolism. I had to get ready for Harrogate and Amsterdam the next day. I arrived at Heathrow at 7:00 a.m. and managed to get through immigration in an hour, a record time for that procedure. I got my case and hauled it down a few flights of stairs to the underground and took the Piccadilly line from Heathrow to Manor House. I usually walk the mile to my home, but I had gone from one-hundred-degree temperatures to freezing in sixteen hours, so I broke down and took the bus. I got into my apartment and watered my little tangerine plant (now an inch tall), did a load of laundry, unpacked, and got ready to review a play that evening.

The August before this trip, when I was in North Berwick, I met a lovely woman, Paula Stotts, who told me she was absolutely sure the people in Harrogate would love my work. She ran events for the local film society and was going to find a way to get me to perform there. Did I know Marilyn Monroe would have been just a few years older than me had she lived, she asked.

I did not.

Several months passed before I got a note from Paula asking if I would do a comedy performance before a viewing of *Some Like It Hot*. I said of course and so the trip to Harrogate, January 31, became a reality. The timing was a bit tight however because I was coming home from Bangkok the morning of the 29th and Paula wanted me to come to Harrogate one day early to have a reunion with all the women who had seen me that evening in North Berwick. Once I began these tours, I decided I cannot indulge myself in jet lag or give myself days to recover from the time changes involved in crossing a lot of oceans. I have jobs to do and commitments to keep.

The morning after I arrived in London, I packed a smaller case for Harrogate and then Amsterdam, and off I went to precede the Blonde Bombshell in her movie and explore one of the most charming towns in the north of England. The biggest adjustment I had to deal with by scheduling a gig in Northern England so soon after I had spent so much time sweating in Southeast Asia was the abrupt change of weather. I went from the freedom of loose cotton skirts to the prison of sweaters, heavy slacks, thickly padded coats, scarves, mittens and hats.

Harrogate is a picture-book kind of place. It has the feel of an old-fashioned English village. One of its highlights is Betty's, a hundred-year-old café that features lovely afternoon teas and beautiful pastries. Everyone in Harrogate loves Betty's, but no one knows who Betty is.

The film *Some Like It Hot* is considered one of the great all-time comedies and Marilyn Monroe in this movie typifies the kind of sexiness that we girls tried to emulate back in my day; sweet, kind and innocent, but hot as a firecracker, out to marry money for security, and hope that love came along with it.

For me, the interesting part of the movie is that Joe E. Brown, the secondary lead in the film, is from Toledo, Ohio, where I was born. His favorite restaurant was my family's favorite as well: Naftalin's. It was the place my daddy took me for my tenth birthday, and I still remember the luscious cinnamon rolls they put on the table for free. Joe E. Brown was Toledo's local hero. Rose Naftalin created a special cookie in his honor shaped like a cigar that he could place horizontally into his very wide and famous mouth. Toledo was so proud of him that they named a park after him. I remember him because I saw him in person on stage when he played the lead in *Harvey*, the story of a man with an imaginary six-foot-tall rabbit. That was the first play I ever saw, and I loved it so much that I have been a theatre junkie ever since.

In the movie I was preceding in Harrogate, Jack Lemmon and Tony Curtis cross-dress. It was the classic *Some Like it Hot.* At the time the film was made, it was very common for men to dress as women for comic effect. My own Uncle Philly danced in a show called the Matzo Ball Revue (really) in a filmy harem skirt with a bangle glittering in his belly button and no one thought twice about his sexuality, including either of his wives or any of his children. They thought he was very funny. Times change and now cross-dressing can often be a statement of gender identity. In this film, and in those days, it was a pure comedy.

At the Harrogate film society event, I was preceded by The Ukulele Ladies, a group of women of a certain age singing ukulele favorites of yesteryear. I did my comedy about what it feels like to be 85 to a lot of people who *were* 85 and all I could think of was why don't they tell *me* how *they* feel. It might add a bit more sparkle to my act.

As always, in these adventures of mine, getting there was part of the drama. Harrogate to Amsterdam was no exception. My flight was supposed to leave at 10:03 a.m. on KLM. I had received no notification of how to check in on-line. Since my printer was broken, I could not have printed anything anyway. I was flying KLM, so I was not worried because they are a reliable, well-respected airline. Had it been Ryanair, I would have been terrified. So, I was up at 7:00 a.m. on a very wintry morning in Harrogate and driven to the Leeds Airport by Brian Madden, a delightful man who collects autographs of famous comedians. Believe it or not, he wanted mine! I signed a book about comedians for him and I was so flattered I forgot that it was 7:00 in the morning – an ungodly hour – and that I had been up rollicking around at 2:00 the previous morning.

When I got to the airport, I was told that because I did not check in beforehand, I was on standby. Brian left me there, after he was assured that this often happens and there is always room on every flight. This time, however, there was not.

KLM apologized profusely for overbooking and sent me in a cab to Manchester to catch a plane at 1:30 p.m. for Amsterdam. On the way there, my cab driver decided to give me a bit of historical background of the area. He pointed out the Rainbow Bridge, the place where everyone in the north of England jumps when life is too much for them. My cab driver noted, with not very well suppressed anger, that when these desperate souls try to jump to their death, they hold up traffic for hours while emergency crews attempt to talk them out of ending it all, at great inconvenience to those who not only enjoy their lives but are on their way home for dinner. I observed that when one has decided to end it all, the last thing on his mind is choosing a time that is convenient for commuters.

I also learned that when God made Lancashire, He made so many mistakes that he was ashamed of himself. He decided to profit from his errors and show England he could do a much better job. "God proved to us that he could do it right when he created York," my cab driver said. I asked him how he knew it was God who did that.

He did not respond.

We got to Manchester Airport and once again I went through security, so KLM could be absolutely sure I wasn't planning to blow up the country. After a long wait, lubricated with a lot of coffee, I finally got on another KLM plane bound for Holland.

To make up to me for the inconvenience, KLM gave me a little package labeled *A Tasty Sandwich* and a cellophane-wrapped biscuit. I saved this for later because I suspected there would be no time for a meal before I had to leave for my gig in Utrecht at Comedy Huis.

I was staying with Edo Berger, who, in my mind, is one of the finest comedians in Amsterdam. He and his wife Nina have just had a little mite of a daughter they named Doris, and I, childless old maid that I am, could not wait to meet her. She had been on this earth for ten weeks and already she figured out the way to her daddy's heart. She smiled up at Edo and gave him a double-whammy stare that would melt a glacier, so grateful is she that he and Nina blessed her with a name she will be able to spell.

I was staying in their cozy guest house and loving the quiet and the privacy of it, after the wild marathon I had been on, rushing from one time zone to another trying to remember which punch line came next and whether it was night or day.

I managed to get myself together quickly (again) and off Edo and I went to Utrecht, a lovely college town filled with bright lights and no parking whatsoever. We finally found a place where Edo could stop the car that was nowhere near the venue. Jurg van Ginkel, the host and funny fellow of the night, came to collect me to walk to the gig. The audience was young, eager to laugh, and very welcoming. The most interesting thing about the gig was that the line-up was all women except for Jurg, who was superb. One of the girls was from Detroit, Michigan, thirty miles from my hometown of Toledo. Detroit is the only place I can think of that is worse to live in than Toledo, so she, like I, got the hell out.

The next night I performed in Edo's room, Mezrab Comedy. I believe that room is the best English-speaking comedy club in

Amsterdam. It is always packed with eager audiences. The last two months were sold out. Edo is a masterful comedian in English as well as in Dutch. My favorite joke of his was when he explained that the Dutch have a saying for everything. For example, if they see someone riding a bicycle into a moving automobile, they have a local saying: Watch Out.

The year before, when I did shows at The Comedy Café, a major comedy club in Amsterdam, I had trouble getting laughs because English is the second language for most of the audience. At Mezrab, although the audience was hugely diverse —Romanians, Russians, Bulgarians, many Dutch people, but younger than The Comedy Café patrons—they were eager to laugh and were very supportive. So again, the evening was a huge success and once again I headlined because one of the other comedians backed out. That made three times on this marathon tour that I graduated to top dog in the line-up. Not bad.

Up at 7:30 a.m., I dashed to the airport and the plane was an hour late. Why was I not surprised? As soon as I got home, my body rebelled. I could almost hear it say to me, "Listen lady, enough is enough. You have dragged me from excessive heat to unbelievable cold. You have deprived me of sleep, and you have not fed me well. I am going to make you pay."

And it did. I got the cold to end all colds. Bed rest, vitamin C and chicken soup. That is what I needed. But that is not what I got. I am a professional comedian, and I had a gig that night in The Phoenix Bar in Oxford Circus in Central London. I was headlining at The Old Rope and the show must go on.

And by gosh and by golly, it did.

***

This was the pace I have maintained since I found that I had to travel if I wanted to perform at enough venues that were willing to book me. By March 2020 I was booked to go to Dublin, Amsterdam, Japan, Ghent, then Amsterdam again, Berlin, Helsinki and Melbourne with gigs each week I was in the UK to fill in the time between trips. And then the Coronavirus swept the world. All my trips have been cancelled and I am now at home live streaming my comedy, writing books and creating another new life again. And why not.

This indeed is what that first five minutes at Cobb's Comedy Club has given me. I am established in my field. I am approaching success. I assure you, I am not there… yet.

It was not always that way. When I was young, I struggled through a childhood with an angry, insecure mother, a vindictive sister and a father too busy to know I existed. It is hard to believe when you see me now, but my every day was riddled with fear.

Dan Dockery took me for a wild bike ride through Hanoi.

I finally got to perform in Paris, another dream come true.
Here I am at Cafe Oscar!!!

CHAPTER 2
How It All Began

My mother was not my friend, but she was everyone else's because she was a conformist who did what was expected of her. I didn't love my mother either, but everyone else did because she was so nice to them. All my mother ever wanted was to have the things everyone in the movies had. She didn't understand that there were no lucky breaks. You have to work for what you want in life. She thought money solved everything.

For example, my mother had a beautiful voice. "I could have been an opera singer if I hadn't had you," she would say. She didn't get that it isn't enough to have a lovely voice. You have to be trained to sing properly and work very hard to become an opera singer.

The reason my mother believed that money was the only ticket to happiness was because when she was little, she starved, and she never forgot that hunger. From then on, she was petrified that she wouldn't have enough to eat. When she was little, she never had a nice dress to wear, and she was ashamed of her clothes until she married my father and he bought her designer dresses. He thought they would make her happy. But my mother was not happy, ever. She married my father because he was a butcher's son and my grandma told her that a butcher's son never goes hungry. But even though she had plenty of food for her tummy, she had none for her heart because my daddy was distant and removed. He was too busy trying to make money for her, so she wouldn't be hungry or ashamed.

My father was not a good-looking man. To me he was God, but in reality, he was a short, very plain-looking man with a bad complexion. He thought my mother was gorgeous. When they went out together, he wore her like a jewel. He was that proud of the way she looked, but he had no idea what she thought because he never asked.

My mother wasn't sure what rich people were like, but she figured if she acted like them, she would catch on. That was why she bought expensive clothes and went to the beauty shop once a week. She had Helen clean her house and Melvin deliver her groceries. She did volunteer work like rich women did, and attended women's meetings, but she never participated in their discussions about social issues. She, like me, was afraid she might say the wrong thing. After all, she was from the class of people those women were pretending to feel charitable about. They were organizing food boxes and clothing that never arrived at her house when she was little, because the really needy people were too proud to tell anyone they needed anything.

My mother wanted me to be "The Perfect Little Girl." She dressed me in hand-me-down clothes because she said that was all I deserved, but she spent a great deal of time braiding my hair and grooming me so I would be clean and tidy. She thought I would play with all the other children and be popular.

Instead, I discovered books when I was two years old and never got my nose out of them. I couldn't bounce a ball. I hated tag. I couldn't ride a bicycle and was afraid of roller skates. I was a social failure, and my mother told me so every day of her life.

The first meal I remember was a glass of milk. I was two years old. By that time, I had developed a mind of my own, and so had my mother. She was a typical Jewish mother. She wanted me fat and compliant so she could show me off to her Mahjong group. My mother sat me in a highchair and locked me in with the tray. She poured a glass of milk and set it on the tray. *I hate milk.*

"Drink your milk."

"No," I said.

"Drink your milk, and I'll give you some tapioca pudding." *I love tapioca pudding. But I hate milk.*

"No."

"Ok, you'll sit there until you finish your milk."

Now, I was used to sitting like this for a long time because my mother thought every child should have one bowel movement every morning. So, at 9:00 a.m. she would sit me on the can with a storybook that she had read to me the night before and leave me there until I did my job. That's how I learned to read.

My mother finished her lunch and went shopping. She left me sitting in my highchair for seven hours. When she came back, she looked at me. She looked at the milk. "Finish it," she said.

"I won't," I said.

At this point, my Aunt Rose came in from the flat upstairs. She looked at me and asked, "Why is the baby in the highchair, Ida? Why isn't she out playing?" She picked me up and kissed me.

"Put her back in that chair. She hasn't finished her milk."

My aunt felt my soggy diaper. It was very lumpy and I didn't smell very good. She put me back in the highchair. She took the glass, smelled the milk, and poured it down the sink.

"This milk is sour, Ida. If you're going to give your kid rotten food, you can't expect her to eat it. Besides, I just came down to invite you all for dinner. I made roast beef and potatoes... and for dessert, Lynnie Ruth, I have tapioca pudding."

She winked at me.

When I was three years old, my parents bought a little Scottie named Annie Laurie, and I adored her. She was tiny and cuddly and sweet. She followed me wherever I went and even stood outside with me when my mother made me go out and play. Our back door had a spring hinge on it, and one day as the dog followed me into the house, I let go of the door too soon. It slammed on Annie Laurie's tail and she began to scream. I was terrified and called for help.

My mother came in, opened the door to free the little Scottie and then turned to me. "That settles it," she said. "You do not know how to care for a pet. I am giving Annie Laurie back to the kennel and you can never have a pet again."

I cried for days because I had hurt a little creature I loved, one that licked my hand and snuggled against me like my mother and father never did. From that day on, I was very wary of all animals, and I was always afraid I would hurt them if they got too near me. My sister was born when I was eight years old, and I was just as afraid I would hurt her because she was little too.

And then when I was seventeen, my mother and father decided to get a wire-haired terrier. His name was William Tell… Junior. This dog was not cute and cuddly like Annie Laurie. He was more like a miniature angry tiger with an attitude. He barked and bit anyone who got too close to him. He attacked every moving thing; and he was so fast he could puncture a car's tires and escape without getting hurt.

The amazing thing was that he and my mother bonded instantly. I think it was because they had the same personality. As soon as Mother walked into the room, Junior would rub himself against her leg. She would pick him up, kiss him and talk to him in Yiddish, "My zyser kop; My lachtican punim. My baby! How can I love four legs so much?"

My sister and I would feel very unloved and deprived because we only had two legs and no fur.

After living with Junior, I stopped being afraid I would hurt him and became really terrified he would destroy *me*. After all, he had torn the postman's jacket, ripped up the milkman's pants, and almost killed the plumber.

But Junior wasn't the only thing I was afraid of.

When I was three years old, the year before we got Annie Laurie, my parents took me to Miami Beach, Florida. My mother put me in a tiny little bathing suit, and she took me to the pool to join my father. My father smiled hello to us both and then he said, "Watch this." He picked me up by the seat of my trunks and pitched me into the pool.

"Oh my god!" my mother said. "What are you doing?"

"Swimming is as natural as breathing to a child that age," my father said. "She'll rise to the surface and swim to the end of the pool just like a fish."

They waited for a few minutes before my mother pushed my father into the pool to rescue me. I had been a difficult birth, and my mother didn't want to lose me that fast. I suspect that in later years she would not have made the same decision.

"Go get her" she commanded.

While Daddy was pumping the water from my lungs, he said, "She must take after you, Ida. Any normal child would have started swimming." I was not a normal child, and I've been afraid of water ever since.

But at that time in America, you were not supposed to graduate from high school unless you could swim. When I was fourteen, I was determined to get out of swimming class. I gave the matter a lot of thought and hit upon my marvelous idea.

On the first day of class, I said, "Miss Peterson, I can't swim today; It's my time of the month." Miss Peterson nodded and sent me up to the balcony where I pulled *Gone with the Wind* out of my book bag and tried to figure out why Rhett Butler didn't give a damn. The class met three times a week and at each class, I told Miss Peterson it was my time of the month.

"Again?" she said. After six weeks she said, "Have you seen a doctor?"

I nodded. "He thinks something's ruptured."

"Oh my God!" she said.

And that was why I was excused from swimming and took volleyball with all the pregnant teenage girls instead.

I wanted a baby more than anything in the world, and I still do, although I have finally figured out this is not a realistic dream. However, even though I had gotten an A in biology, I didn't really understand the exact procedure that would get me one. I was desperately jealous of those girls in volleyball class. I'll never forget the look on their faces when I pointed to Salina's tummy and asked, "Oh my god, how did you do that?"

When I was eight years old, my sister was born. She was a colicky child who screamed day and night. She exhausted my mother, and because Mother was always so tired, I couldn't seem to do anything to please her. So, whenever I could, I escaped to my grandma's house. I adored my Bubbie. That is what I called her, and she called me Leenie Rute. The minute I walked into her house, my cheeks bloomed like roses and my ebullience bubbled like champagne. Any food she set before me was heaven. "Eat, Leenie Rute," she would say, and I gobbled up anything she gave me because her food tasted so delicious to me. I don't believe there was anyone in my life I adored as much as I did that tiny woman who smelled like starched clothes and a bakery. I was certain that she was God. She was the only person in the world that I did not fear.

Picture this: I am nine years old. I am sitting in the brand-new house my father bought for my mother because she always wanted to live in a gated community. I'm reading *They Love to Laugh* by Kathryn Worth (my favorite book).

I escaped my mother by reading books… All kinds of books.

"Go to bed," my mother says. I hear her, but I don't move. I continue reading. "GO TO BED NOW!" my mother says.

My heart is pounding. My mouth is dry. I close the book. I walk as slowly as I can and climb the stairs to the second floor of our home. I stop in the bathroom to change clothes to get ready for bed and I realize… I have to get my nightgown.

"LYNN RUTH!"

Time has run out. I creep down the long dark hall and pause at my bedroom door. I take a deep breath, but I can't do it. I know they are there waiting for me at the window. I know it and I am afraid.

"Lynn Ruth! Are you in bed yet?"

I turn my head, so my eyes are pinned to the left, away from the window, but when I turn on the light, the mirror on my dressing table defeats me. And there they are! Grotesque, wiggly squiggly creatures are dancing on the darkened window waiting to grab me. I am too terrified to scream. I switch off the light. I trip over a pair of shoes and slip on a petticoat, but I manage to grope my way to the bureau to get my nightdress and then scuttle down the hall back to the bathroom. I brush my teeth and then my hair. I wash my face.

"Lynn Ruth!! Why aren't you in bed yet?"

I feel my way down the hall and manage to get into bed in the dark. I pull the covers over my head and shut my eyes, but I can't fall asleep. I can feel those horrid creatures waiting for me. The minute I turn on the light, they will be there!

That was more than seventy years ago. It took me years of living and learning to realize that those creatures in the window were me. I was afraid of my own reflection. I am in my eighties now, and when I look in the mirror, I am not at all afraid. I am horrified.

Fear was my constant companion in my childhood. I was afraid of bullies because I knew they would always win.

Our first house was a duplex, and the caretaker of the building lived downstairs with his wife and two children. His son, Dale, was a short, stocky kid with dirty blonde hair and a bad attitude. He loved to pick on anyone weaker than he was and when discovered me, he found his perfect target.

My mother read in a child-rearing book that children needed fresh air every day. I hated to go outdoors because I was afraid of all the other kids. They screamed and chased each other and stepped on my toes. Sometimes they pushed me over, and I skinned my knees. I pleaded with my mother not to send me outside, but she was unmoved. Every day, she would dress me in a spiffy hand-me-down from my rich Aunt Sally and push me out the back door. "Go play," she would say, "but don't get dirty."

And that was where Dale found me. He would be sauntering home from terrorizing Carol Reinstein or Marcia Zimmerman. He would stand so close to me that I could smell the chocolate bar he stole from Marcia on his breath and he would spit at me. Then he would spit again. I'd continue standing without moving until my mother would call me for lunch. I never told her what Dale did. She would have just gotten angry.

Here I am in my spiffy hand me down from my rich Aunt Sally.

One neighbor liked to sit at the window when she did her nails, and one day when she was giving herself a manicure, she witnessed this little drama. She waited for me to react and when I did nothing, she leaned out the window waving her newly lacquered nails at me. "Lynnie Ruth! Don't let him get away with that! Spit back!"

And now the tears poured down my face. "I can't," I sobbed. "I can't spit straight."

"You stop that," she said to Dale.

"Make me," he said.

"I certainly will," She said. She picked up the telephone and waved it in the window so he could see. "I am calling the police." But she didn't call the police. She called my mother. "Lynn Ruth just stood there," she said. "Why didn't she fight back?"

My mother had a little talk with my father. "Someone has to teach that child to spit back," she said.

"You do it, Ida," my father said. "I don't believe in confrontation."

"Do you want that little shit to beat up your daughter because she doesn't have the guts to give him what he is giving her?" my mother said.

My daddy *really* didn't like confrontation, especially with my mother. "I guess not," he said, and he took my hand. "Lynnie Ruth, come with me," he said. "I am going to teach you to fight your own battles."

"What are battles, Daddy?" I asked, and I followed him into the backyard.

My father was a mystery to me. He came home at night and read the paper, but he never said hello to me or asked how I was. The only time I ever heard his voice was when my mother spoke to him, and she used the identical tone with him that she did with me. It was *Why are you late again?* Or *how am I going to explain to Peggy that you won't go to her party?*

It sounded exactly the same when she corrected me. She would scream *Eat your spinach*; Or *Don't dawdle!* to me in that same tone. So, you can imagine how exciting it was for me when my Daddy took my hand and spoke directly to me in his quiet, very daddy-ish voice.

He could have mashed me to the ground, and I would have been thrilled. But of course, he did no such thing. He was a gentle man and was careful not to step on bugs or hurt flies. It was my mother who smashed beetles and swatted mosquitoes. My father took me into the backyard, and he formed my hands into a fist. "Are you ready?" he asked.

I had no idea what I was supposed to be ready for, but I was determined not to lose this beautiful moment with my father. "Yes, I am," I said.

"I am going to hit you, and I want you to hit me back," my father said.

"Was I naughty?" I asked.

"No, of course not," my father said. "I am going to hit you so that you learn how to defend yourself. OK?"

Well, hitting me was better than ignoring me, so I was ready to be brave and take it. I nodded. My father reached out and tapped me on the cheek. When he stooped over so I could reach him, I thought he wanted me to kiss him, so I did.

"No!" my father said. "When I hit you, you need to hit me back. Now let's try again."

He poked me in the tummy, and it tickled. "That was fun!" I said. "Do that again."

"It's no use," said my father, and took me back into the house. "She's not the type," he told my mother. "She's not a fighter. She is a lover."

But I wasn't that at all. I was too afraid to love anyone. I didn't trust them enough.

That is why I never thought happiness was for me. All the things I really wanted never happened. I wanted to be married; I wanted children; I didn't want to go through this life alone. Those things never happened for me.

When my rich Aunt Sally had a baby, my mother took me to the hospital to meet him. In those days, you were in the hospital for two weeks. "Hello Lynnie Ruth. Meet Brucie," Aunt Sally said.

I had never ever seen anything as adorable as Brucie. Even Annie Laurie paled next to this precious baby with rosy cheeks and soft down on his head. I wanted to take him home more than anything I had ever wanted before, and my mother thought that, when she turned her head, I would grab Brucie and run out of the hospital with him.

"You can't have Brucie. He belongs to Aunt Sally," she said.

My aunt reached down and took my hand. "We can share Brucie, Lynnie Ruth." she said. "Now stop crying and give him a kiss."

And I did.

But all I could talk about on the way home was how much I wanted a Brucie of my own. My mother decided to get me a teddy bear to stop my begging and when she gave it to me, she said. "This is YOUR Brucie."

I was thrilled. I loved that teddy bear like nothing else in the world because it was the first real gift my mother gave me, and I dragged him with me everywhere. I refused to part with him until I was eight years old and my teacher explained that it was so crowded in our classroom, and I would have to leave Brucie at home to make room for a real child. Well I did leave him home and as the years went by I was so busy growing up that I forgot about Brucie. Still, the idea that I could never have anything that made me happy stuck with me for way too many years.

I was always afraid I would say the wrong thing and make people angry. When I was tiny, every time I said something my mother didn't like, she would say, "Watch your mouth or I will send you back to the American Indians. You will have to live in a teepee and wear feathers and all you will eat is corn."

I hate corn.

Despite her warnings, I have been walking around with my foot in my mouth ever since my mother decided to drive my aunt, my cousin, and me through America's deep south to Miami Beach, Florida, so she could practice feeling like an aristocrat at a fancy hotel.

In those days, there was no air conditioning in automobiles, and my cousin and I were in the backseat of our Buick, the brand-new fancy car my father had bought for my mother to go with her designer dresses. The windows were wide open to let in some air. As we drove through the beautiful fields of cotton everyone sings about, I saw hundreds of tiny little children out in the hot sun picking cotton instead of going to school and learning how abused and diminished they were. This was before Martin Luther King and Rosa Parks had tried to convince American farmers that black people deserved equal rights. When I saw those little children, I thought they were adorable. They had those cute little pigtails with bright ribbons on them. I leaned out the window and pointed to one child in a red dress who was just about my age, and I screamed in a voice so loud you could hear me three states away, "Look at that cute pickaninny!"

"That is a disgusting thing to say," said my mother and she and my aunt hunched down in the car so low it looked like no one was driving. My mother sped through Georgia and Tennessee at approximately 100 miles per hour, terrified we would get lynched.

As the years went by, my parents' social pretensions often got me in trouble. At one point, my mother and father decided to join a country club in Toledo, so they could see how the upper-class lived, a status they seemed to want more than they wanted happiness. My mother made the mistake of taking me into the ladies' locker room. I had never seen a naked body before. Our family was the kind that undressed behind closed doors, always. When I saw all those half-naked women, I was amazed at how different their bodies were from mine. I was after all only seven years old. I pointed to one buxom lady and shouted, "What are those things hanging from her chest?"

The years have not lessened my penchant to come to inappropriate conclusions, and I do not want to discuss how many times I have asked a portly young woman when her baby is due, but I have to say that the most humiliating incident of all happened when I was eighty-one years old and had just moved to Brighton, England.

I love little babies. The minute I see one, I gallop over to get a closer look and automatically compliment the mother even if her child looks like a caged monkey. I was on my daily walk when I saw a lovely pink and white carriage with twinkly bells and rattles hanging from the hood. I peeked inside and its contents were swaddled in a blue blanket, and its face concealed by a yellow bonnet. I reached inside the carriage to pull away the blanket to get a closer look at the adorable little person inside. I cooed and gurgled as we adults do because we actually believe babies like hearing incomprehensible sounds. I was all ready to tickle that child's chin when the resident of that buggy barked at me and sunk its little teeth in my thumb. Without thinking, I turned to the lady pushing the carriage and said, "How adorable. She looks just like you."

All my life I have been terrified of authority figures. I believed everyone was stronger and knew more about everything than I did. And I always knew that if I didn't do what they said, I would get hurt just like Cinderella did when she was mouthy to her stepmother.

And then I met Harold.

Harold was the most important authority figure in my life so far. When we moved to our fancy new house, in Birkhead Place he was the policeman who stood on Cherry Street and stopped the cars so the children could cross the street to go to school. Every time I saw him, I put my little hand in his very big one and say, "Hello, Harold."

Harold would say, "Hello, Lynn Ruth, are you ready to go to school?"

And I would say, "Yes, I am."

Then Harold would carry me piggyback across the street! I loved that so much I wanted to go back across the street so he would do that again. And that is why I thought all policemen were angels who would hold your hand and carry you across the road. To me, every policeman was a friend I was not afraid to love. After that, whenever I was in trouble, I always called the police for help and they never disappointed me.

I loved all my teachers and they loved me. Except one. Miss Fox. I was determined to make her like me, too, but it was an uphill battle. Miss Fox thought I was manipulative, fawning and weak. She did not like me at all. She wore the same outfit every day—a navy-blue skirt, red jacket and white blouse, with her hair tied up in a bun. She carried a box of tissues with her because she sneezed all the time. She sounded like a trumpet that had not been tuned. When she reprimanded one of us, she always said, "You look at me when I speak to you."

She taught speech and I was in her class. No matter what topic I chose and how well I memorized what I had to say, Miss Fox found endless fault with me.

One day, she caught me whispering to Billy Kalb and sent me to the principal's office to sit on the naughty bench. I had never been punished in school before, and I was petrified because I didn't know what happened to bad children. The principal was a marvelous human being, a spinster who devoted her entire life to loving other people's children. Her name was Susan Godfrey. She took me, sobbing and shaking, into her office, listened to my story and said, "Lynn Ruth, when people treat you cruelly, did you ever think they may be hurting inside? Maybe Miss Fox has something in her life that makes

her unhappy, and that is why she is often very strict and
unbending to you."

I nodded and left the office feeling very sorry for Miss Fox.
Then I thought, "What about me? I'm hurting inside, too."

And then I had my marvelous idea.

The next Friday I had to give a speech. I turned up dressed
in a navy-blue skirt, a red jacket, a white blouse, my hair tied
back in a bun, holding a large box of Kleenex. "Hello," I said.
And I sneezed. "Today, I am going to tell you how NOT to give
a speech. You look at me when I am speaking to you."

I sneezed again and blew my nose and looked at Miss Fox,
expecting her to send me to the naughty bench. But she was
laughing, and we were friends for the rest of the year. We even
invited her over to our house for dinner.

My mother loved to cook, and her happiest moments were
when someone ate her food. There were only four of us. She
was always on a diet herself because she was so short that one
brownie increased her hip circumference at least five inches…
or so she said. My father had ulcers and barely ate anything.
My sister was so fat my mother couldn't cram her into ready-
made dresses so my mother limited her intake. That meant she
had only me to stuff with her marvelously exotic soups, roasts,
casseroles and desserts. I was the perfect target: I was so
frightened of her that my metabolism was locked into survival
mode, and I burned food as if it were kindling.

My mother's signature dish was spaghetti and meatballs so rich that one spoonful would give a hippopotamus indigestion. It came with huge slabs of garlic bread drenched in butter and was followed by a sumptuous, whipped-cream pineapple custard angel food dessert. One slice of that cake would satisfy 500 starving Armenians, but my mother expected us to eat it after we had downed all that spaghetti, immense meatballs bigger than a bull's *cajones* and enough slabs of bread to fill a bakery.

Most of her guests collapsed after the first plateful of spaghetti. My father didn't bother to address it at all. My mother served him a poached egg on toast. My sister was allowed one small serving, although she lusted for more. That left me, and I rose to the challenge. I ate and she smiled. I ate and she let me go to a party. I ate and she didn't scream. I ate all of that food. Every single time.

When I was twelve years old, I had the starring role in my piano recital. I wanted my mother and father to come to my performance more than anything in the world because I thought that would make them think I was wonderful. I put on the very first dress I had that wasn't a hand-me-down. It was pink with white bric-a-brac, and I brushed my hair until it was very shiny. I felt beautiful.

I put on my coat and asked my mother, "What time will you get there?"

"I'm not going," she said. "Why should I? You haven't done anything for me lately."

I was devastated. I walked the two miles to my piano teacher's house fighting back my tears. When I played "Humoresque," I didn't make any mistakes, and my teacher said I was marvelous, but I didn't believe her. I knew I didn't deserve to be the star of a recital because my mother didn't think so, and she knew me better than anyone.

Back in the forties, a girl's sixteenth birthday was a huge event. Most of my friends were given big parties on that day, and Normie Odesky's daddy took her to the Kin Wa Lo nightclub to celebrate. Normie got to wear high-heeled shoes, nylon stockings, and real lipstick.

My father had scheduled major surgery the first week of October, so my mother told me they would not be celebrating my birthday that year. I loved my daddy, but I was pretty sure the feeling wasn't returned. When he would see me on the street, he couldn't even remember my name. He would look at me and snap his fingers and say, "Hello…Princess." I knew he knew my mother's name because he would always shout, "Ida, can't you keep those two girls quiet?"

I came downstairs to breakfast on my birthday and my mother was dressed to go out. "They finally took all the tubes out of Daddy," she said. "I have to go to the hospital."

"Does that mean he can come home soon?" I asked.

"Maybe. Your orange juice is on the counter and there might be a cinnamon roll in the bread-box," she said, and then she was gone.

As soon as she left, my favorite cousin Murray called. "I just realized this is your birthday, Lynn Ruth!" he said. "Do you think you could stand going out for dinner at the Hillcrest with an old man like me?"

"Oh wow, would I!" I exclaimed, and then I remembered that I was sixteen and no longer a child. I cleared my throat. "How lovely of you to remember me! I would love to join you."

Well, I don't know how thrilled Normie was when she went to that nightclub, but I do know that *I* could barely sit still with excitement. I had a date with a twenty-year-old man. This was maturity!

Murray picked me up at 6:00 that night and we drove downtown in his yellow Ford convertible. My cousin took my hand and led me to the elevator. "The dining room is in there," I said, pointing to the large area on the other side of the door.

"This was such a special occasion that I reserved us a table in The Tower Room," Murray said.

I could hardly believe it. The Tower Room was where important celebrities who came to Toledo ate...both of them. When the elevator opened, there was Normie and all my friends waving banners and balloons. "HAPPY BIRTHDAY, LYNNIE RUTH!" they said, and I began to cry.

"Did you plan this?" I said to Murray, and he shook his head. "Your mother did."

I was stunned. I didn't think my mother would ever do anything special for me, especially when she was so involved with Daddy and so I began to cry again.

Well, the meal was delicious, and I blew out all seventeen candles (one for good luck) on my chocolate cake.

"What did you wish for?" Murray asked.

"I wished that my daddy would get well," I said.

The band began to play "Deep Purple" and Murray nodded. "Let's dance," he said.

We walked to the dance floor, and Murray pointed to the door. It opened and there was my father. He was very pale and stooped over as he walked over to me and held out his hand. "Happy Birthday, Princess," he said. "May I have this dance?"

My mother had driven my father to the party. She followed him into the room, and I saw her there after Daddy and I had finished our dance. "Happy Birthday, Lynn Ruth," she said.

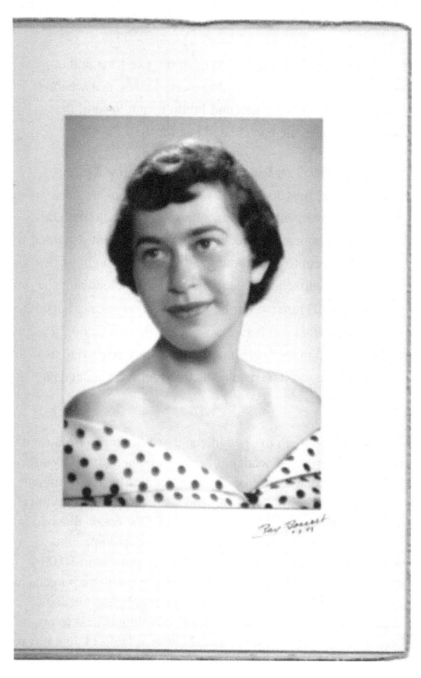

*I was the dreamer in the family...always hoping my mother
would love me.*

"Thank you," I said. I was overcome with tears and too frightened of her to say anything more. I knew that whatever I said would ignite her anger and I didn't want to spoil the beautiful bubble she had created just for me.

As I look back on that magical party, I realize that my mother was as tongue-tied as I was. She was not an introspective woman, and I am sure she simply did not know how to communicate her feelings to this intelligent daughter who didn't seem to care about the things she thought were important. I realize now that my mother didn't hate me; she just could not figure me out. She was far too insecure herself to try to remedy this gap between what she thought I should want and what I did indeed care about. She simply refused to deal with it or with me. The result was that I felt very inadequate and unloved.

I decided to go to The University of Michigan because it was a well-respected academic school. I began university life in Mosher Jordan Dormitory, and I hated it. My first roommate was Phyllis Milgrim, a maniac who had every kind of mythical disease you could imagine, and she drove me crazy. She had to have quiet when she was in the room. I couldn't open the windows, even when I was suffocating. Lights out at 10:00 even when I still had studying to do. There were two bureaus in the room, but I couldn't use either of them. Phyllis needed them for her clothes. I had to pile my belongings next to my bed. It never occurred to me that she was at fault. I knew it was me. My mother had told me so.

I decided to join a sorority and chose Alpha Epsilon Phi (AEPhi) because it had a reputation for high intellectual standards and excellent cuisine. It was there I met Cathy, who cooked gorgeous meals just like my mother. Cathy would leave all the leftovers from our dinners for us girls to eat when we came home from our dates after the 10:30 p.m. curfew. We devoured endless cupcakes, custards, pies, and cream puffs washed down with cups of cocoa topped with marshmallow fluff and moaned about the gorgeous men who didn't notice us and the disgusting ones who did.

I met Ginger that first year in AEPhi. She was a little redhead from Ashtabula, Ohio. To my amazement, she asked ME to room with her the next year. I couldn't believe it. "Oh, you don't want to room with me," I said. "I am impossible."

"No, you are not," Ginger said. "You are the most possible person I know."

And so, it was, I roomed with Ginger my junior and senior years. We spent a lot of money and time decorating our room to make it beautiful. We bought a corner desk so we would get good light when we studied, and we bought big band posters to decorate the walls. We painted the walls a warm ivory color and bought matching spreads for our beds and pretty curtains. "Why are we doing this?" I said. "It is only a room."

"No, it isn't," said Ginger. "It is our home."

While we lived together, I learned about respecting preferences. Whenever Ginger went on a trip, even for a weekend, she took at least ten outfits and I would say, "Why are you taking so many clothes?" and she would say, "I don't know what the weather will be." As soon as she got into a hotel room, she unpacked everything and moved the bed away from the window so the light wouldn't disturb her. I would say, "Why are you bothering to do all this? You are only going to be here for a day." and she would say, "Because I like it that way." A phrase I had never, ever had the courage to say.

I met Bobby Golten when I was a sophomore at Michigan. I don't know if I was *in love* with him, but I know I loved him because he paid attention to me. He looked just like Howdy Doody, a famous puppet on TV at the time. Bobby was 5-foot-5 with red, curly hair and lots of freckles just like the famous puppet. He liked me because I was shorter than he was and I never said no to anything he wanted to do… except sex. My mother had convinced me that sex was a lethal criminal act that would mutilate my future and lock me into a home for wayward girls the minute I succumbed.

I did not succumb.

I didn't really understand men anyway. Men were shadowy creatures who stood up when they urinated and played contact sports. I realized, however, that I would have to connect with one in some mysterious way if I wanted a baby.

My body developed into a reasonably shapely female form but didn't function like other girls. I was in biology class one day when we read about hermaphrodites. After I read the description, I decided that it explained why I was so slow to develop. I couldn't wait to call my mother to tell her that because of her genes, I was physically stunted.

When she heard the word hermaphrodite, she thought it was some horrid, degrading, and disfiguring disease that would make her look bad at family gatherings. She called our family doctor, Myron Fink to discuss this new revelation. One thing led to another and the next thing I knew I was in Michigan University Hospital undergoing surgery for ovarian cysts. If I thought the surgery was unpleasant, it was nothing compared to the new way of life it created. I was now a victim of cramps, mood swings, and monthly bleeding that was inconvenient, uncomfortable, and ruined a lot of underwear.

In short, I was a woman.

I was always a romantic. I believed in the tooth fairy, wishing on stars, and true love. In those days, when we went to college, men wanted letters after their name and women wanted them before theirs. Ginger had two men who wanted to marry her. Two. I had none. She married the man who could support her financially. I graduated with honors, single and loveless. All I had to show for my degree was a teaching job in Cleaveland.

Valentine's Day. 1956. I bought fifty Valentines to send to every man who had ever showed me the slightest bit of attention. At three cents a stamp and 25 cents a card, I invested $14 in finding myself a husband.

There was Jerry the Candy Man. I loved him because he bought me Bavarian crèmes and had a gorgeous standard poodle named Bon-Bon. Jimmy, the guy from Monroe I should have married because he was sweet, kind and loving; he just didn't turn me on. Bob who was drunk, very exciting, and decidedly unavailable. Mike, who hung from the engineering archway to make himself taller and Bobby Golten, even though I knew our liaison was over. Ronny and I wore out the telephone chair talking to each other in my senior year in high school. Buddy was the first man to notice the curves in my sweater. Jay took me to see the Kafka classic, *Metamorphosis*. I was so horrified by the movie that I didn't even notice Jay. All I wanted was to get home and hide under the covers.

Then there was Mr. Preston, my ex-music teacher and Dickie who used to come over to the sorority house to watch me walk down the stairs in my pegged skirts. Joel Friedman was the one person who got about as close as anyone did to teaching me how to swim. I spent the most glorious summer lying in his arms in the pool, kicking and blowing bubbles in the water while he held me up, my tummy resting on his hand; And Tommy Treeger, Ginger's cast-off boyfriend.

In each note I said, "Hi. I am teaching in Cleveland and thinking of you. Will you be my Valentine?" It took me three hours. I had writer's cramp for a week. I knew it was a gamble, but I had to do something, didn't I? I was twenty-two years old and single, for God's sake. If I didn't find someone in a hurry, I would end up an old maid, baby-sitting other people's children and knitting afghans for the needy.

Despite the initial success of the operation to turn me into a woman, my body was determined to stay a little girl. The doctors gave me female hormones to get me back on a female track. The hormones made me retain water and so for the first time in my life, I was putting on weight, and I didn't know why.

I was invited to a Valentine's Day party and decided to buy a new dress. I had always prided myself that unlike my mother and my sister, I stayed skinny, no matter what I ate. I walked into a dress shop, pulled a few size sevens off the rack and tried to get into them. Too tight. I worked my way up from seven to eight to nine to ten to eleven to twelve. I finally managed to cram my bloated figure into a beige number with a relaxed waistline and a full skirt.

I came home, got on the scale, and I was horrified. I had always fluctuated between 98-103 pounds and now the scale told me I weighed 127 huge, fat pounds. I was becoming my mother and my sister! This must not happen. I looked at my fat self in the mirror and I said, "You will lose 25 pounds by the end of March. Period." And so, I dieted and dieted and dieted some more.

While this battle with my bulges was going on, I received a letter. It was from Tommy Treeger. He had received my valentine and was coming through Cleveland on his way home from Korea. Could I meet him at the airport? He would like to take me out for dinner. I was so excited, I got scarlet fever.

I wonder if that was why I married him.

My first wedding in September 1956. 22 years old and filled with hope.

I figured out that I didn't love him well into the engagement, but I knew that with my history of failed or non-existent romance, this was as good as I was going to get. I determined to make this marriage work. I made up my mind to be a model wife. I finally experienced sex in a motel in Indiana, and it was a nightmare. And I said to myself, "Is this what I saved myself for?"

I found myself cooking, cleaning, teaching school, trying to live on almost no money at all, frightened of food, frightened of angering Tommy in case he would hit me again, frightened of life. And that was when the eating really got out of hand. I bought a Waring blender. I blended ice with instant coffee and vanilla and lived on that for days while I created gourmet meals for Tommy and his fellow students at Harvard Business School. But after I starved for a week or ten days, I broke down. Late at night while Tommy was asleep, I crept into the kitchen and consumed everything in the refrigerator: A pie, a slab of meat, a pound of butter, a loaf of bread, a bowl of whipping cream. I didn't know why I was eating like that, why I couldn't stop.

One day I had invited four couples over for dinner and decided to make chocolate icebox cake for dessert. I went to the A&P and bought six one-pound bars of semisweet chocolate, whipping cream, lady-fingers and a dozen eggs and smiled at the checkout girl. "I am making a chocolate icebox cake!" I said. "Sounds great," she said. "That will be $7.85."

I drove home with the groceries in the front seat beside me. By the time I got to the first traffic light, I had eaten all six chocolate bars. I turned the car around, bought six more one-pound bars of semi-sweet chocolate and smiled at the checkout girl. "I decided to make two of them," I said.

I finished those chocolate bars before I got out of the parking lot. "The hell with it," I told myself. "I am making a lemon cake." And I did… and I didn't eat it until dinner was over, my guests had left, and Tommy was asleep.

The marriage lasted two years. But even worse than Tommy leaving, I had to go back to live with my mother! "I knew it wouldn't last," she said. "Go set the table."

She had made a three-rib roast, potatoes, and cauliflower. I sat down at the table and ate all the cauliflower, most of the potatoes, and the entire roast. My mother, who had never seen any human being devour food that way, said, as I reached for the slab of fat remaining on the platter, "For God's sake, save some for the dog!"

"All you ever think about is that damn dog," I cried, and I stormed out of the dining room.

The next morning my uncle called. "I have a baby for you, Lynn Ruth!"

A baby? My uncle was a lawyer. My mother must have told him I was having trouble conceiving and asked him to find a baby for me that some poor girl couldn't keep. Why couldn't she leave me alone?

In those days, your life was over if you didn't have a husband. My life was over, *and* I was living with my mother. So, I decided it was time to end it all. This was a challenge because I hated blood and I couldn't stand pain. I gave this new project a lot of thought, just like I had the swimming problem and the Miss Fox challenge. That was when I got another one of my great ideas. I bought four books, *To Kill a Mockingbird*, *East of Eden*, *Not as a Stranger,* and *Valley of Decision*. I put them in my Renault and drove it into the garage. I closed all the windows and doors, turned on the motor, and began reading. It took me two months to finish the books and still I was alive.

This approach was obviously not working so I tried to gather the courage to slit my wrists. I just could not do it. Instead, I drove the car to work at 90 miles per hour without stopping at any intersection and prayed I would either be arrested or demolished. Either way I would be out of my mother's house. One day, my mother said, "I know what you are doing, Lynn Ruth. Keep it up and you will become a paraplegic, and I will have to care for you for the rest of my life."

That ended the suicide attempts.

Instead of dying, I went to Toledo University and got a master's degree in Creative Arts for Children. While I was studying I was also teaching second grade at Elmhurst school. I was twenty-five years old. The principal was Edna Breed, and she treated the children like objects instead of people. That year, I taught a child named Bobby whose mother took in customers during the day while Bobby was in school because it was the only way she could pay for his clothes and his lunches. (That means she was a prostitute.)

When Bobby came home from school, he would often have to wait outside until his mother's customer left the house. He was an emaciated child who wore glasses thick as Coke bottles. He was a behavioral nightmare, and it took all my patience to deal with him. He was unruly and angry all the time, and I had to protect the other children from his unreasonable rages. However, I understood why he was so conflicted, and I knew that love and understanding was the only thing I could give him.

One day, I stayed home from school with the flu. The next day, when I entered the classroom, the children couldn't wait to tell me what had happened. "Mrs. Breed hit Bobby with a ruler!" they said.

I looked at him and he nodded. "The substitute teacher sent me to the office because I bit Caroline," he said.

"That wasn't very nice for Caroline, was it," I said. "I think you'll have to sit next to me for the rest of the term." Caroline sent me a relieved look and Bobby was happy because he could sit at the front of the room and feel important.

My life so far had taught me that you have to stand up for what is right. You have to protect the underdog… not just for them, but for yourself. After school, I marched into Mrs Breed's office. "How much do you weigh?" I demanded.

"135 pounds," she said. "Why do you want to know?"

"Good for you," I said. "Bobby weighs 37 pounds and you smacked him yesterday. Do you feel better? Because I can assure you, you didn't do a thing to help that child." And I walked out of her office.

I was fired at the end of the year. Some things are more important than keeping a job.

They say that timing is everything, and I assure you it is. I was walking past a CBS TV station one day when I was twenty-seven and decided to go in to talk to the manager. He happened to be sitting at his desk wondering how to get some free public service programs on his new station. I marched into his office and said, "I just saw *Romper Room* and it was a piece of trash."

He could not figure out what I was doing in his office, but he didn't like what I just said. So, he said, "Oh? I suppose you can you do better?"

"Yes, I can," I said. "I have a master's degree in Creative Arts for Children."

He paused and then he said, "Ok, if you can find a sponsor, I will give you a program."

I got the Toledo Art Museum to sponsor me, and I got the program. On the day of the first screening, Paul, the engineer, offered to drive me to the station. My experience with any man having control over me was horrifying, but this time I thought, "What have you got to lose?" I took my knitting as a shield and off I went in Paul's car to the viewing room. However, before we got there, a woman test-driving a new car drove into the passenger side of the car, and I went through the windshield (no safety belts and no safety glass in those days). My shoes landed on the doorstep of Toledo's only nightclub, a forecast of what was to come.

The next thing I knew, I was shivering uncontrollably and a man with the sweetest voice ever was saying to me, "Almost done and you will be as beautiful as ever." The man was a master plastic surgeon who happened to be on-call the night my face was sliced off as I soared through the windshield of Paul's car. I also broke my arm, loosened all the muscles around my eyes, and fractured several bones in my foot... but I didn't hear that bit of news until much later.

"I'm cold," I told the doctor.

"We will get to that later," he said. "Right now, I have to save your ear."

"My ear?" I said and then I passed out.

I really should have died that night. But I didn't. It took a while, but I recovered, and the television program ran successfully for two years.

It took another year to completely get well, but once I was healthy I went out on a blind date with a man from Columbia City, Indiana, and it turned out I was the one who was blind. I was a moral young lady of the 1950s. The man, whose name was Richard Flox, seemed to like me. He read poetry to me and took me out for several lavish dinners. Then he asked me to marry him. By that time, I had given up the idea of love. Richard offered me a house of our own in his little town along with financial stability. I accepted and we married. We did not have sex while we were engaged because proper young girls in my time did not do that.

I was aware that he was not very amorous during our courtship, but it was on our honeymoon that I realized that he was not interested in sex with me at all. I was coming to terms with this when one day my father appeared in my kitchen as I was preparing Richard's lunch and said "Pack your bags. I've come to take you home."

"This is my home," I said. "And I am busy. I have to get Richard's lunch ready for him."

"Richard is not coming home," said my father. "He called me to come get you. He cannot stand you."

What I did not know was that he wanted a wife to be a front of respectability for him. He was gay and having a torrid affair with the local doctor. And so, the marriage was over. I was back in my mother's house defeated, once more.

*I didn't bother wearing white for the second wedding. We said
our vows in my parents' living room. Here they are hoping to
be rid of me at last.*

CHAPTER 3
California Dreaming

I felt totally lost after my second divorce. I had tried not once but twice to live the dream I was told should be every girl's nirvana. My mother and all the world told me so. I married despite my doubts because I thought marriage was the only decent life for a woman. I ended up emotionally and physically bruised and battered. I finally understood that I needed to change my goals if I wanted to live any kind of a satisfying life. My old patterns of behavior and the way I made decisions were not working for me.

I decided to create a whole new life, one that had the elements in it I really wanted, not the ones I thought I should have. I applied to Stanford University to get a degree in journalism. I had always wanted to enroll there but was too afraid to apply because I was so sure I wasn't smart enough. But after those two soul-shattering messy divorces, I threw caution to the wind. I sent in my application; certain it was a waste of time. To my surprise, Stanford accepted me.

Myrtle, one of the office workers in my father's firm, offered to drive me out Route 66 to Palo Alto and get me settled. I loved Myrtle. She was a no-frills, no-fuss, down-to-earth person. The two of us had a wonderful time driving through the desert and up the coast to my new home.

I found a cement-block studio apartment adjacent to Highway 101 and a ten-minute drive to the university. Myrtle stayed long enough to be sure I was settled in with linens, dishes, a bed, a table and a chair. Then she flew back to Toledo, and I was alone. I knew no one in Palo Alto or at the university. No one at all. I was terrified…but determined.

I needed to create a brand-new, successful Lynn Ruth Miller. I was done with the one who failed at everything she tried. Others didn't think I was a failure because all they saw were my high grades in school, the children who loved me as their teacher, and my reliability and honesty in everything I tried to do. None of those things felt like achievements to me. All I saw were conflicts with a demanding principal at the school I taught in, and all the people who got higher grades than I so easily when I had to work so very hard.

I realize now that we are the only ones who can define our success or failure. I did not believe in myself. So, whatever I did was never good enough. I can still remember when my first husband left, and my neighbor knocked on the door as I was packing up the few things I needed to go back to my mother's. She was an elderly woman, and a kind, sweet, human being. "How could he leave you?" she said. "You baked a challah every Friday night. You lit the candles."

And I said, "I think there is more to marriage than a loaf of bread."

Now, I had a third chance to change direction. I was determined to succeed at Stanford. I believed it was my last chance to make something of my life. Until now, I had been an insecure, frightened human being who used her brain to second-guess what everyone expected of her. This was my opportunity to pull out of the cocoon I had created for myself. If I failed this time, I would end up a total nothing. This time, I must make my brain work in more creative ways. This time, I would become a reporter for a newspaper. I would stop being a charity case, always out of money and always one breath away from tears. This time would be different.

I worked day and night, studying, going to classes and creating a "string" (the series of articles you showed to newspaper editors to prove you could write a presentable story). My major was journalism even though I was sure I was already a great writer. I had been writing poems, essays and newspaper features since I was ten years old.

After I graduated, I was jolted into reality when Dr. Rivers, my wonderful and inspiring professor wrote in his critique: "When I first read Lynn Ruth's writing, I thought there was no hope, but I have to say I have never seen anyone work as hard as she or be as open to criticism as she was. She has become an outstanding writer."

And I thought I already was.

I graduated top of the class ten months early. I was triumphant. Surely with such high scholastic achievement, I would get the position I wanted at a salary that would support me. How could I not?

But reality was not as kind to me as I expected. Although I tried and Stanford Employment Center tried, I could not find a job. After my stellar graduation, I ended up selling Golden Books in Macy's toy department during Christmas…a temporary job and certainly not what I had worked so very hard to achieve. I stayed in San Francisco applying for jobs until I finally realized that no one there would hire me. I decided that I had to be realistic and leave the place I loved so much because I could not support myself there.

I went to New York because I was told it was the center for journalistic employment. I spent six months applying to every possible writing outlet, and I got no positive response from anyone. And that was when I fell apart. I was thirty-two, and I had failed again. I call my father to come get me. I returned to Toledo, tail between my legs, a total failure. I had no money. I had no hope.

As I sat in my father's car, I told myself somehow, some way, I would get back to California. It was where I belonged. I just had to keep trying. That is typical of the way I think. I believe in what Henry David Thoreau said: "If you have built castles in the air, your work need not be lost; that is where they should be. Now put the foundations under them."

It took me sixteen years filled with false starts and missteps, but I never lost sight of that dream. I finally managed to return to the Bay Area and my version of paradise. During that time, I became a college professor and acquired two cats, two dogs and a string of feature articles published in magazines and newspapers to prove I could write.

Stanford had not been a waste of time. I had learned how to write for publications. It was just that no one wanted to pay me for what I did. I managed to buy a mobile home of my own by saving pennies from a series of part-time jobs. I took workshops in painting and became an artist in oils and acrylics, but I still could not support myself. I had no job security and ahead of me loomed a bleak future, a black cloud of poverty and despair.

My parents had been singularly unhelpful during my years of struggle. They had had enough of this crazy daughter who never made anything work for her. I rode a rollercoaster of dashed hopes and shattered dreams, and they refused to climb aboard. I knew I was the only one I could turn to if I needed help.

I did not like my sister, and she did not like me. When I look back on our relationship, I realize now that I was desperately jealous of her because my parents treated her very differently than they treated me. To me, she was fat, lazy and demanding. She was a liar with no compassion for anyone but herself. Yet, it was my sister who got to buy expensive new clothes whenever she wanted them. I wore my cousin's hand-me-downs until I was fourteen and then I was allowed only the cheapest additions to a very sparse wardrobe.

She went to a private school. I begged to be allowed to attend that school, but my mother told me I wasn't smart enough. My sister married and had children. It was my sister who lived in a lovely house in suburban Toledo. I lived in a lower-class mobile home park with blue collar workers who had no concept of what it was like to be part of the educated middle-class.

My sister never managed to get a college degree; I graduated with honors. My sister never went out on all the dates I did, nor was she invited to the many parties and social events. She was never president of her sorority or in the top ten of a graduating class.

I was.

I know now that my perception of her success and my failure was in my mind. In reality, my sister had to cope with immense prejudice because she was obese. She had a very high IQ but was unable to apply herself to her studies. My mother was determined to protect her from rejection and believed that if she sent her to a prestigious private school and dressed her like a fashion model, people would not be cruel to her. I still remember years later, when my wise friend Ellen said, "Sibling rivalry is always caused by the parents." It suddenly became clear to me that my hatred (because that is what it was) of my sister was nothing but envy because she got the love and protection I never received from an insecure mother and a father determined to buy his way into society's elite.

This is not to say my sister was blameless. She figured out that she had an edge over me very early in life. As a child, she would accuse me of abusing her when I had done nothing at all, and my mother would punish me without even listening to my defense. I never fought back because I considered Marsha Dee beneath contempt. And that made her even angrier.

I will never forget when my sister's marriage ended. I was living in my mobile home with barely enough money to feed myself at that time. She called me and said, "I never want to end up living the kind of life you live."

And I thought, "I didn't want to live this way either, but it was you who got the support and the love I never got. It was you living in a lovely home and getting help from our parents and then alimony from your husband. I never got one penny from my first one and my second one sent me $125 a month for two years. That was barely enough for food."

I now realize that this very neglect and lack of support is what made me strong. I understand now that I cannot make people love or help me. I needed to find the inner strength to make the life I want. At the time, I felt like all I did was beat my head against a brick wall, but I understand now that I was chipping away at walls that I myself had built. My parents, my sister and the world didn't care if I failed or not. They were far more dedicated to creating their own successes. I was not important to them. So, I needed to be important to myself.

I also knew that my health was precarious. What had begun as a passive-aggressive way of fighting back at my mother blossomed into a vicious, uncontrollable eating disorder. I resented my mother's immense, and what I thought was unreasonable, power over me. I know now that I allowed her to have that power.

Her passion was cooking. The one way I could hurt her was to refuse the beautiful food she prepared for us each day. My alternating anorexia and bulimia accelerated when I married and then one day a doctor said, "You know there is a name for what you're doing: anorexia nervosa."

Once I realized that the starving and stuffing syndrome, I was living had nothing to do with hunger, I was determined to control it. I refused to allow myself to have a mental disorder. It took superhuman effort, but gradually my fixation with food was not so apparent, and I thought I was healed.

I know now I was not. I believe I tussled with food fixations for at least forty years, never admitting I had a problem. When my life became too turbulent, I descended into some kind of harmful eating pattern just hovering on the edge of a visible disorder.

My body stopped functioning when I was thirty-six, and I believe it was because of what I had put it through from the time I was sixteen. I stopped absorbing food, and nothing the local doctors did stopped my decline. Even though I was eating, I was dying of starvation. That was when one of the doctors realized that I had early-onset osteoporosis.

I was reading *Time* magazine in a medical waiting room one day, when I saw that Dr. Frederic Bartter at The National Institutes of Health (NIH) was seeking participants in a study of young women with osteoporosis. I wrote the doctor, and he answered by return mail. In January of that year, I went to NIH as a part of that study, but once there, the good doctor tried to figure out why the food I was eating was going through me like a sieve. Despite my gargantuan appetite, I was dying of malnutrition. I was put on a six-week metabolic diet: you eat the same three meals every day with meat from the same animal.

But because I ate so much, by the end of the fifth week, I had devoured all the meat they had set aside for me and they had to start again, kill a second cow and corral another flock of chickens! My stay was extended to twelve weeks and beyond because no one could figure out how to keep food in my body.

I traveled a roller coaster of hope and despair for more than four months until, at last, I ripped the plastic I.D. bracelet from my wrist and insisted an attendant wheel me into a taxi bound for the Washington, D.C. airport and home.

"You can't leave NIH yet," the head nurse said. "If you do, you will be dead in two weeks. Every bone in your body will break."

I looked at this well-meaning young lady and I said, "Arlene, I am having too much fun here. I have never had so many people pay so much attention to me in my life, but there has to be a better way to get that kind of attention than by being sick."

So, I left the hospital. I weighed less than 55 pounds. My legs were like toothpicks; my eyes hollow caverns and my skin transparent. I looked like a centerfold for *World Health* magazine. My parents, who had written me off months before, barely hid their dismay at seeing this wraith that had once been their daughter land in the Toledo airport. They deposited me in my mobile home to expire.

The week I got home, my mother, who never believed I was really sick, called. "While you were gone, no one did my garden," she said.

So, I did what I always did. I obeyed. I got into my car and drove the equivalent of the distance between Brighton and London and did her garden. I drove home and pulled to a stop at a huge intersection behind a cement mixer. Because I was so weak, I coasted into the truck and my head hit the steering wheel. "Thank God! It's over," I said.

After about five minutes I thought, "Death has to hurt a lot more than this."

I got out of the car fully expecting to fall onto the pavement in a heap and instead, the only thing wrong with me was a bloody nose. The car was not so fortunate. The entire front end was smashed. "You may not be much," I said, "But you are better than anything General Motors can make."

I drove home and said to myself, "Lynn Ruth, if you really want to get well, you are the only person who can make that happen." And then I thought, "What did the caveman do to get well? He didn't go to doctors; he ate good food, exercised, and breathed fresh air."

I decided to heal myself with common sense and old-fashioned remedies. I knew that exercise was what I needed, but I hate exercise. I thought maybe I should get a puppy to walk to force myself outside in Toledo's horrid unpredictable weather.

That was when I remembered Annie Laurie. I didn't live in my mother's house anymore. I could get whatever I wanted in my own home. I determined to get another Annie Laurie to love. I still lived at the mobile home park, and I was walking down the path to the main house with my little six-year-old buddy, Bobby, and I said, "I have decided to find a fuzzy puppy to love."

"We have a futhy puppy," said Bobby. "Theba had babies."

"Sheba is a terrier," I said. "She would not have given birth to a fuzzy puppy."

"Yes, she did," said Bobby, and he took my hand. "I'll show you."

We walked into his mobile home and there was Sheba, with three sleek baby terriers and one very fuzzy puppy. I named him David and took him home to love. It was David who showed me that dogs are like people. Some are lovely and some are horrid, and some get their tails caught in doors because they are stupid. That is why I am not afraid of animals now… except for the two I married.

Here I am with David, the true love of my life.

That year I returned to NIH for another two-month stay and then ended up in Henry Ford Hospital for another month. Each time I left the hospital I swore that would be the last time I would let my body rule my life. I never gave up and never stopped believing I would eventually be fine. It took nine years for me to get well enough to function. By that time, David was looking both ways before we crossed the street and had the slimmest hips in town. I was walking nine miles a day; my edema had vanished, and I weighed ninety pounds.

I had chosen to live.

During that year in and out of hospitals, no one was able to diagnose the cause of my physical decline. I always feared that whatever had triggered my breakdown would happen again and I had to be prepared to deal with it. That can be a frightening thing when you are alone and ignored by your family.

But for me, it was empowering. Whenever my father had come to my rescue (and he had done it numerous times), he always reminded me that I was an unwanted burden to him. Each thing he did to salvage the wreckage I had made in my life was riddled with his recriminations. I was filled with guilt and smothered in an overpowering sense of failure. In contrast, when I set about finding my own way to take care of myself, I felt liberated and strong.

While I was at NIH, they put me through innumerable tests to try to understand why my body rejected food. They were never able to isolate a cause. The doctors said I could never work again, and it was their diagnosis that got me a pension from the Ohio Teacher's Association when I finally left the hospital. I have always believed I got well because I had the security of knowing there would always be money for food and shelter.

The amount of my check was about $350 a month, and it became a pseudo-parent to me. When I used it, I wasn't as humiliated as I was when I had to accept my father's begrudging help. The money barely covered my cost of living, but I supplemented it with freelance articles, babysitting, and odd jobs. I also learned to live on very little. Even today I would not dream of taking a taxi or paying for a ticket to see a movie or a play. I do not buy clothes unless I am desperate, and then I go to charity shops. Economy is a way of life for me and because of that, I have always saved enough to have a cushion in case of disaster.

I was barely well enough to live a normal life when I left Toledo for a job in Oklahoma City writing for two magazines and a newspaper. I drove my two dogs and two cats across the country in a Pontiac station wagon and worked for a woman who demanded I work almost twenty-hour days. When I finally realized I could not handle the demands of the job, she fired me. That was when I decided to travel around the country writing stories the way John Steinbeck did in his bestselling book *Travels with Charlie*. (Charlie was his poodle.)

I said to myself, "Steinbeck is a man with one dog; I am a woman with two dogs and two cats. I can do what he did and do it even better." I traded everything I had accumulated in my six months in Oklahoma City for a GMC truck and a fifth-wheel trailer that was hitched to it. It took another six months for me to learn to drive the rig, but by September, one year after I had left Toledo to make a life for myself, I was on the road.

I traveled alone with the dogs and cats out of Oklahoma to Nacogdoches, Louisiana. I spent a week there. Then on my way to Hot Springs, Arkansas, I got stuck in Winnie, Louisiana, because I crashed the rig and broke all the brake cables. I got out of the truck with the dogs and a young man called Glen who had been watching this little tragedy said, "You are in trouble, aren't you?

"I sure am," I said.

"I'm going to help you," he said.

He took my keys, and with the dogs yelping beside me, drove us to an RV shop. The mechanic informed us it would take at least a day to rewire the trailer and the young man smiled at me.

"Well," he said. "Guess that means you'll be spending the night with me." I opened my mouth to object, but he silenced me. "I'll just put these little fellers in the back seat, ma'am," he said. "You get into the front there, and we'll drive over to tell my wife you're coming home with me. She works nights at K-Mart."

The drama of the next few hours happened over thirty-five years ago but its wonder still amazes me today. We stopped at K-Mart first to meet his wife. "This here is Kate," Glen said.

He explained my predicament and Kate smiled at me. "Of course, you'll stay with us," she said. "We would just love to have you."

Glen drove me to his home and made me dinner. While it was cooking, he helped me shampoo the dogs. Then he put a mattress on the living room floor for him, his wife and the three children. I slept in the master bedroom. By eight o'clock the next morning I was on the road again and a man I had just met was waving to me as if he had known me all his life.

"How can I thank you?" I asked as I settled into the driver's seat.

"I just did what needed to be done," he said.

I started the motor. He waved goodbye to me.

"Love you," he said.

I continued on my travels through Arkansas, Louisiana and Texas. I stopped for a month in Laredo, a town on the Texas/ Mexico border, and every day I would see tiny little VW campers drive across the border, open the back door and fifty Mexicans would fall out onto the ground. Laredo was a beautiful place where people of a multitude of races worked together and respected one another. However, my job there was to guard a junkyard, and while I was doing that, the place was pilfered almost every week. My employer was a friend, and he didn't exactly fire me. He just told me there was lots more to Texas than Laredo and kept hinting I should do a bit more exploring. Then he told me I might like the Texas Hill Country.

I drove that 24-foot rig into Wimberley, a tiny, sleepy little town that at the time could not have had more than 1,200 residents. Half of them worked in Austin and the other half didn't seem to do much except sit around talking or smoking pot.

The first three months there, I worked as a counselor at The Rocky River girls' camp to earn my rent and utilities. The camp closed in September, and I had nowhere to go. Two teachers had a home nine miles from the town center and taught in Austin all week. They asked me to watch their home while they taught. I took the job because I had no real choice. When I drove out to that property, I was alone in the wilderness with no telephone, no radio and nothing but my two dogs and two cats to keep me company.

In those next four months, I learned to love my own company because I had no one else. I learned to take care of myself, eat proper meals, exercise and stretch my mind. I wrote endless stories about nothing much. I went out every day to walk the nine miles into town and back again that evening.

Gradually, I made friends along the way with people I never would have met if I had lived the life my mother had told me I should. Most of these Wimberley people were high on drugs, and many were squatters who lived on other people's property. Yet, they had wisdom and perspective I knew nothing about. They invited me to dinners they created out of found food, or we sat around playing music and singing.

It was very, very hot in Texas that year. I used to fry eggs on the doorstep and put a kettle in the sun to make it boil. I wore a pillowslip instead of shorts and a top because it was so hot, I wanted to get out of my skin. One day, I was walking down the road, when a policeman stopped me and asked me to please walk on the side of the road because I was holding up all the trucks and creating a lot of road rage. I said, "What do you do to people who cause road rage here in Texas?"

And the policeman said, "We shoot them." That was when I figured out that the police in Texas weren't like Harold or the policemen I knew when I was a youngster in Toledo Ohio. They were definitely not my friends. I moved over to the side of the road.

I continued walking to the community meeting place, the Blue Hole, where everyone was so high on pot that all I had to do was inhale to feel good. I laughed and sang with everyone. My dogs played with the other dogs sitting around the quarry, and I tried to get the resident parrot to talk to me. I had the best time the year I spent in Wimberley because I learned that being me was enough.

I had to leave my job because the two women decided I was a lousy watchman. They had more robberies in the three months I guarded their house than in the five years they had lived there. They lost a lot of china, silver and furniture, and they blamed me for it. Broke, ashamed and desperate, I called my father (again). "I can either eat or pay rent," I said. "I don't have enough money for both.

"I am sending you $500," my father said. "Get the hell out of Texas."

"I will," I said. "I am going to California."

"Why do you want to go to a place with the highest cost of living in the entire country?" he said.

"Because the only time in my life I was ever happy was when I was in school at Stanford University."

And so for the first time in my life, I gathered enough courage to disobey my father. I drove my camper truck out to Redwood City, California, a place halfway between Stanford and San Francisco and pulled into a trailer park on December 23, 1980. The woman in charge said, "You can stay here tonight, but you have to leave tomorrow. It's Christmas Eve, and we're fully booked."

"They said that to another nice Jewish girl," I said, "And you know what she did. She had a child who started a whole new religion."

Well, I did not start a new religion, and I did not have a baby. Instead, I met a woman who was running a magazine dating service and needed a telephone operator to take calls and fix up men for sex, and she gave me a job. I began my new and beautiful California life at 2021 Glendale, my very own tiny house. I had received three years rent credit and a Valiant to drive in trade for my RV and GMC truck. Marvin, the man who owned the dating service, had always wanted to go camping and I no longer had use for my rig once I landed in California. That meant I did not have to pay rent, a blessing because my $350 pension barely paid for gasoline and food.

My tiny house was in a mixed neighborhood of non-conformists, and I fit right in. Next door was a group of Hell's Angels; behind me, a house of prostitution. The boy living in the house on the right was a pseudo gun-toting cowboy who did target practice in his backyard (adjacent to mine) at every hour of the day or night. Down the street lived a magic Filipino lady named Lourdes who played classical music at top volume while she tended her garden. I passed her home every day on my way to work at the dating service with my three dogs: Jake, a nervous wreck of a cocker spaniel, Cindy, my special darling who had traveled with me from Toledo to Oklahoma, through the southwest United States to Texas and then to our final destination in California, and Molly, a tiny mutt I rescued from the trunk of a car in Oklahoma City. I always stopped when I got to Lou's house to discuss whatever was playing on her radio.

Even though I had some very difficult times settling into my new state and creating some kind of solid base for myself, nothing tarnished my happiness. I was where I wanted to be, and I knew somehow the rest would fall into place.

Day by day, I began making contacts and enlarging my circle of friends. I became an usher for the San Francisco Opera. I often took Lourdes with me so she could enjoy the music she loved, and see it performed live on stage. I was introduced to a whole community of people who worked behind the scenes and front of house for bay area performances when I went to a play produced by The Menlo Park Players. I spoke to a delightful English woman named Anne Vaughan and explained that I had very little money but wanted to attend theatre as much as I could. She said, "You know, we always need backstage help at this theatre. Why don't you volunteer?"

I started as an usher who helped people to their seats and graduated to helping with the props they needed for their productions. It was because of that job that I gave up smoking. I had smoked unfiltered cigarettes since I was thirteen. It was my addiction, a prop that saw me through twenty years of that severe eating disorder. I tried to curb my smoking at NIH and by the time I got to California, I was down to four cigarettes a day.

I was doing the props for the play Cactus Flower at Menlo Park Theatre and they needed a pack of cigarettes for one of the characters. At the time, I had a severe cough and cold. However, I was determined to smoke my four cigarettes no matter what they did to my throat. As I tried to inhale, coughing and gasping for air, I said to myself, "This is ridiculous. You are killing yourself for no reason. You do not need that cigarette. You just think you do." I put out the cigarette I was smoking and drove the rest of the pack down to the theatre. I never smoked again.

Anne Vaughan became a mentor for me. She was ten years older and a hundred years wiser than I. She was always there for me if I was in any kind of trouble, and it was she who paved the way for me to become part of this vibrant, cultivated, and very interesting new community: the people who usher and work behind the scenes at the shows you see.

It was in Menlo Park that I met Gerry Fox. He had escaped Germany right before the Second World War and had become an engineer for United Airlines. He was married to Rosalie, a Holocaust survivor who had been hidden in a basement in Holland during the war. They became close friends, almost family to me. Gerry adored classical music and because of him, I became an usher for the San Francisco Opera and saw all the great operatic stars on stage. I met Placido Domingo in his dressing room. He was a true Italian gentleman and thanked us all for visiting him when we were the ones who should have been thanking him for such a beautiful performance.

My most memorable opera experience was meeting Patricia Racette, the lead in *Madame Butterfly*. She was in her mid-thirties at the time and always brought her poodle to wait in her dressing room while she sang on stage. Butterfly is a fourteen-year-old innocent child in that opera, and the middle-aged Racette became that child bride when she was on stage. It was a magical performance that I still thrill to remember.

Ushers for the San Francisco Opera were not paid when I was there in the eighties and nineties. All those who helped out Mrs. Beverly, the head usher there, loved the opera. The chance to see these beautiful, lavish performances not once but several times was our payment. However, when Willie Nelson came to the Opera House, Mrs. Beverly could not find anyone to take the patrons to their seats. I volunteered to find her people to work the aisles and brought them up to San Francisco from Redwood City in a caravan of cars. We turned the opera house upside-down with a bunch of down-home, plain-talking country-western fans singing "On the Road Again" as we helped people find their seats.

The eighties marked the beginning of the AIDS Crisis and San Franciscans suffered cruelly. Henry, the man who signed us in as ushers, used to sit in a drafty hallway with a scarf around his neck. Each week I could see him diminish. I liked him very much. There was something very kind and sensitive about him. I would always ask him if he was all right and if I could help him, but he brushed aside my concern. And by the end of my first year, Henry was dead.

I can still remember going to hear The Gay Man's Chorus at Christmas and seeing men so frail and wasted that I couldn't believe they could stand, much less sing. It was a terrifying time, and one that taught me how cruel homophobia could be. I remember going to a play about a Rotary member who died of AIDS in Los Altos, a wealthy community south of Palo Alto. The woman sitting next to me turned to her companion and said, "Those people are disgusting," and her friend said, "If he had had tuberculosis, would you say that?" (The man in the play who contracted AIDS was straight.)

When I married a Richard Flox, in 1959, our marriage ended in three months because he told my father he was gay. I always believed he had chosen to be homosexual. My parents believed I was the injured party in that relationship (the only time they thought I was not to blame for one of my failures). Richard had used me to cover for him and maintain his place as a respected member of the community. The truth was that I would not have left him because I wanted marriage at any cost. I never understood why he could not simply live alongside me. We could have carried out the façade of man and wife.

It was during this time in San Francisco as I watched beautiful, kind men I knew who shared my passion for the arts die before my eyes that I finally understood the fear and torment Richard had suffered. In the late 1950s, gay men were given shock treatments to "cure" them. If he had "come out," he would have been hospitalized and ostracized. Right about that time, one of my fellow ushers and I were talking about how difficult gay relationships were, and he said to me, "Do you think I would *choose* to be a victim of all this prejudice and anger?" And it clicked. I understood. And I cried for him and for everyone who does not fit into the box society has created of acceptable people.

Despite my living in the place with the highest cost of living in the United States, my own cost of living was practically nothing. I never paid for entertainment. I met a sister of The Sacred Heart, Jane McKinlay, at a folk dancing class. It was right about this time in the eighties that nuns stopped wearing habits and Jane told me the hardest decision she had to make every day was deciding what to wear.

She was very aware of my financial limitations, and so every six months when the sisters cleaned out their wardrobes and discarded what they no longer wanted to wear, Jane would drop off a bag of clothing for me. I was very well-dressed thanks to the sisters and very grateful.

CHAPTER 4
The Attack

It was my own personal horror story, and I will never forget its lesson. I thought I was living in paradise. I ushered for every cultural event in the Bay Area and filled my evenings with classical music, fine drama, and dance. I worked at a telephone service during the day and did research for the Political Science Department at Stanford. I could hardly believe how delightful my life had become. "This is what middle age should be," I told myself. "I have finally found the road I need to follow."

Then, at 10:00 on a Saturday night, I decided to walk the dogs one last time before I went to bed. I clipped their leads to their collars and flipped the porch light on. "Ready?" I asked. They wagged their tails. I reached into my pocket and gave each a biscuit. "Mama's darlings," I said, and I smiled. "Off we go!"

When I returned, I took a hot bath and got ready for bed. I wrote in my journal and then picked up my book. The dogs were flat out at my feet. I rubbed Molly's ears. Cindy stretched and moved to my lap. Jake rolled over and began to snore. I kissed Cindy's head and the dog snuggled against me. I adjusted the lamp and lost myself in the story. A young man was trying to outwit the FBI and the mafia, and it looked like he just might succeed. My eyes devoured the pages.

I read for three hours and forced myself not to flip to the end. I reached for the light switch and paused. I was hungry. I put on my robe and took my novel into the kitchen with me. I hadn't had time for a proper dinner, just a sandwich and coffee, and I was famished. The dogs padded after me into the kitchen. I leaned down to pet them. "And biscuits for you!" I said. "I promise."

I pulled out a casserole of turkey from the refrigerator and put it in the oven. I plugged in the coffee grinder on the counter and spooned out some coffee beans. The tiny kitchen bubbled with the rich brown aroma of the casserole and perking coffee. And then I heard footsteps outside my door. I was furious. "Who does he think he is? Why does he have to cross my back porch to go next door? What's wrong with the street?"

I could hear the clatter of heels as he climbed over the fence, and I yanked the back door open. "You get out of there!" A man stood before me, a giant shadow in the doorway. I froze. I tried to push the door shut. Too late. He grabbed me by the collar and hit my face. My head snapped to one side, then the other. I stared at his blurred image, horrified. His features were stone.

"Why are you doing this?" I screamed. My voice gurgled in my throat and my words died. I heard the thud of my body as it fell to the floor, but I felt nothing. "I don't even know you. You are a horrible dream. Yes. That's it. Any minute I'll wake up and you'll be gone. You're that dill pickle I couldn't refuse. Do you understand? YOU ARE NOT REAL!"

He struck me h... again and again. I crashed into the
Tiffany lamp. It ...ed to the floor in a blue shower of
broken glass. H... d my collar like a leash to lift me above
the debris. Hi... hand smashed into my face. Once more, I
tried to scre... ut my voice froze. My body was a bundle of
white-hot ... "Stop! STOP!" The words rumbled like phlegm
in my th... My eyes filled with blood. It poured down my
face an... aked into my robe. I could taste it, acrid and bitter.
Awfu... *Oh God, please make him quit. Why are you letting him
do th... to me? He's going to kill me.*

He dragged me across the floor. My hips bounced against
the hardwood boards. The jagged edges of the broken light
bulb ground into my legs. My slipper caught in the heat vent. I
could feel my ankle twist as the shoe wrenched from my foot.
My eyes refused to focus. The room whirled around me like a
movie reel escaping from its spool. The dining room table
danced on marshmallow legs; the living room couch squashed
into a misshapen ball.

My robe twisted and my collar tightened around my throat. I
gasped for air. My eyes bulged and my tongue filled my mouth
like a saturated sponge. He pulled me into the bedroom. "No!
No!" At last, my voice worked. It sounded like a warped
record; a wild banshee wail. I could hear it accelerate into
knives of sound that sliced the blood-thickened air.

He stopped. He stared at the three dogs sitting silent on the
bed. They were hypnotized by the repeated thud of my head
against the bedroom wall. He threw my limp body aside. "Oh,

the hell with it," he said. I crumbled to the floor and skidded in a pool of blood.

He turned and wiped his hands on his pants. I stared, immobilized as my blood spread across his black corduroy slacks. He tore open the bolted front door as if the locks were paper. He was gone.

I stumbled to the telephone. *Got to dial operator. Got to get help.* I heard a cracked, frantic voice force itself out of my throat. "I've been attacked. Oh, help, someone. Help. 2925 Glendale. Hurry. Oh, please hurry."

Did that tinny sound come from *my* throat? Impossible. I dropped the receiver. I stared at red-streaked walls and carmine pools splattered across the floor. "Must clean it up... now." I staggered into the bathroom and wet a towel with cold water. My blood fell into the sink and spread like batik dye. I looked up into the mirror. Who was *that*?

A grotesque mask stared back at me; its right eyebrow pulled halfway to its hairline. Its nose was bent almost flat. Its mouth was frozen into a tight, pursed knot. Blood dripped down its lacerated chin. *That* couldn't *be me!*

I got down on my knees and wiped up my footprints even as fresh blood fell to the floor. I held another rag to my face and washed the telephone. I soaked the stained towels in cold water. I rubbed them with soap that burned into the abrasions on my hands. I scrubbed until the stains disappeared down the drain. I plugged the sink and soaked the towels again. Then I remembered dinner. I forced myself to hurry into the kitchen. I turned off the oven. Sirens. "Thank God."

I weaved into the living room and clutched the couch for support. The room whirled around me like a crazy Ferris wheel. The broken door was still ajar. Through a veil of blood, I saw the two policemen enter. I staggered across the floor into their arms. I could smell the freshness of outdoors on their rough wool coats. I clung to them and tried to speak. It was no use. I'd lost all my words. All I could give them were tears. Wild, gasping sobs.

"All right, lady. Try to calm down. Tell us exactly what happened. What did he look like? Have you ever seen him before?"

I shook my head. "He was dressed all in black like a silhouette, and he smelled like…" I frowned, puzzled. Then I nodded. "He smelled like jasmine, that's it, just like those bushes in Charlotte's front yard. He pushed his way through my back door and hit me." I swallowed hard. My eyes darted from one man to the other, and I gripped their sleeves. "Why did he do that? I don't even know him. He dragged me into the bedroom, and I thought… I thought…" I looked up at the men, and my eyes overflowed. I paused and swallowed. "Then, he stopped."

"We're going to take you to the hospital. Someone needs to look at you."

I shook my head. "I want to go to bed. I'm so tired... *so* tired."

"Lady. Your face won't wait. You might get some kind of infection. Where is your coat?"

I grabbed my purse and hesitated. I reached for my book. This might take a while, and I was almost finished with the story. The two men helped me out the door. I heard the screeching sirens and felt the jolt of the squad car as it tore through stopped traffic. Then the world went black.

The hospital doors opened. I clung to the two policemen. The tiled floor undulated like a distorted ocean. My legs were foam rubber, my eyes warped glass. I turned my head away from the light. "I'm so cold, so cold," I said. I tried to focus on the scrambled panorama before me. The place was electric with activity. Masked figures in white, bustling women with pink-striped dresses, attendants pushing wheelchairs, interns waving charts, moving, always moving. The antiseptic smell choked me, and I felt as if I had been dumped into a freshly scrubbed latrine.

A wheelchair whizzed so close I curled my toes. A baby cried. A woman burst out of one of the curtained partitions. I held a cloth to my mouth and fell against the reception desk. A man carried a screaming child in his arms. The little boy kicked and pounded his fists on his father's chest. The child's shoe flew across the room. It bounced on the wheel of an empty gurney and landed on the floor, a tiny, red sneaker, bulging at the toe, run down at the heel. It lay on its side, empty and unnoticed. I felt blood trickle down my forehead. I looked for the policemen. "I want to go home." I said. But the two men had vanished. I was alone.

I watched the medical staff rush past me. I tried to grab a sleeve, an apron, a glance. "Please, let me lie down." My knees felt like melting Jell-O. I reached for the wall. I touched the cold plaster and felt myself drift out of reality. And then, as if by magic, I was the center of activity. A face appeared. A hand took my arm. Efficient people propelled me into a screened-in cubicle and drew the plastic curtains. A nurse removed my clothes.

"Oh dear," she said. "I'm going to have to pull this off. It's stuck to your skin. You poor little thing." *Don't feel sorry for me or I'll start crying, and I must not do that. I must* not. The woman tied my hospital gown. "All set, darling. Dr. Winter will fix you all up good as new." The nurse stroked my hair and smoothed it away from my forehead.

More tears. God *damn* the tears. They made me feel helpless, weak. "I'm terribly cold," I whispered. Blankets. Hot water bottle. Maternal clucking.

"Doctor will be right in, love," said the nurse.

I was alone again. I groped in my purse and found the book. I opened the pages and the print dissolved into rivulets of ink across the page. I closed my eyes. My pulse thundered in my ears. My head throbbed, and my leg looked like raw meat. I hadn't even noticed my leg before.

"My goodness! You look awful. Sorry we couldn't get to you sooner. Had a baby in convulsions and a motorcycle crash just before you got here. Crazy, isn't it? Quiet as the morgue all night and then at midnight, all hell broke loose. Must be a full moon." *What? Oh, yes. This one was a doctor.*

"I didn't see the moon." *Or the stars or the road or anything but flashing lights and the blood that filled my eyes.*

He had a stethoscope around his neck. He was two darting irises and a green mask. I looked at the receding hair, the creases in that forehead and tried to reconstruct a face. It was no use. His fingers probed my forehead and then pulled back the flesh. "Looks like you bumped into an angry Mixmaster."

I shut my eyes and saw his face, a stone mask, silent, cold, evil. I shivered and shook my head. "Not quite," I said. He smiled, and I became a person once more.

"Hold still," he said. He poked at my face with gentle fingers, careful little touches that pushed my features back where they belonged. "I'll have to take stitches in this eyebrow… your leg, too. Your nose is pretty bad."

I smiled. "I can still smell," I said.

"That's not what I meant."

He paused and pushed the bridge of my nose. "I think I can straighten it,"

"That hurt."

"It's all over. You're pretty as a picture."

"That's a switch. I was a middle-aged disaster before."

"My God! A comedian! I can't believe it!"

I couldn't believe it either. Why this sudden euphoria? I felt full of fun, *fun*, for God's sake. I chattered, I quipped, I laughed and entertained. I was the star of the night. I looked at the clock on the wall. 3:30 a.m.

"You sure there isn't a full moon?" he asked.

"Positive." I returned home at 4:00 in the morning, exhilarated still. I thanked the police who drove me from the hospital. I kept talking in a wild attempt to keep them with me, but it was no use. They left me at my front door, and I was alone. Except for the dogs. They barked. They bounded to me and licked my feet, jumped for my face, rolled across the rug. "Why didn't you do this when HE was here?" I asked.

I sat down on the floor and let them love me. I took Cindy into my arms and buried my face in Molly's fur. "My babies. My wonderfuls. Oh, my little loves!" More tears. Would they never stop? I stood up. "That hurt." I pointed to the bedroom. The three dogs trotted over to the bed. I leaned against the door and felt a hundred years old. The place was chaos. My heart walloped my ribs and my head felt like tissue paper. I forced myself to concentrate on one action at a time. I moved slowly and methodically to set things right.

I propped a chair under the doorknobs of both doors and looked once more at the debris. I sighed. I picked up my purse from the floor. I hung my coat in the closet. I scraped the dried blood from the carpet, the walls and the telephone. I soaked more rags and rinsed out the ones I had used earlier. I sat down and tried to center myself. "What was I doing before HE came?" I looked around the tidy room. My eyes rested on the table. It was set for a meal. "That's it. I was heating turkey."

I got up from my chair and forced my legs to take me into the cramped Pullman kitchen. It was still warm and smelled of food. The coffee pot was cold to the touch. I lit the flame. I looked at the door. It had scuffmarks and streaks of dirt and blood. I sprayed it with Windex, and it was clean. I tested the knob. The door was locked. I leaned my forehead against the wood panels. I had wiped out the visible remains of the attack, but how could I erase this terror? Windex couldn't do *that*.

I pulled my casserole out of the oven. It smelled like comfort, and I wanted it. "No use going to bed, now," I told the dogs. "I'm too wound up." I pulled off bits of meat for Jake and cut up the liver for Cindy and Molly. "Dog biscuits for dessert," I promised.

Molly lapped at my ankle. I knelt beside my fuzzy puppy and buried my bandaged face in her silken fur. I felt the solidity of the dog's body and that was real. Jake licked my face, and I could feel his sturdy ribs and steady heartbeat. That, too, was real. Only this night was a mirage, an endless black fantasia. I clung to the puppy in my arms. "Oh, lovey," I said. "Oh, my lovey."

I stood up and put on my apron. I worked in the kitchen by rote, soothed by the routines I knew so well. My breathing slowed, and my thoughts centered on my task. I set my book on the table and read as I ate. I washed the dishes and let out the dogs. I swept the floor and scoured the sink. I undressed and brushed my teeth. I opened the medicine cabinet door so I wouldn't have to see my face. I opened the back door. "Bed!" I called.

I propped the chair under the doorknob and secured the chain bolt. The three dogs hopped on the coverlet, and I crawled under the blanket. I nuzzled my face into Jake's black fur, and I closed my eyes. It was 6:00 Sunday morning. I slept until Monday night. I felt swollen, lumpy as a bag of potatoes. I went into the bathroom and looked in the mirror.

Who was *that*? Two black eyes, a bandaged forehead and a broken nose. Black and blue smudges, yellow, red and purple marks, cuts, scabs. Pain. *Oh, my Lord. How can one body ache like this?* I turned away and reached out to open the bathroom door. Suddenly, the dogs burst into a cacophony of sound. They barked, yelped and squealed. I took a deep breath. *He was out there. He has come back to finish the job.* I felt myself shrink into a terrified knot and I pulled away from the door. Then I stopped. I put my hand back on the doorknob. "That man has taken over thirty-six hours of my life from me," I said. "I am not giving him one minute more."

And then I did the bravest act I have ever done before or since. I opened the door. "Come on kids," I said to the dogs. "We're taking our walk."

CHAPTER 5
Transitioning

When my three-year lease was up at 2021 Glendale, my landlord told me I had to leave my sweet little house because his brother was coming to Redwood City from Mexico. By that time, I had three dogs—Jake, Cindy, and Molly—and three cats —Eileen, Sarah, and Toby Anne. Many California landlords do not accept pets, and I could not find any place I could afford that would allow me to have animals. These pets were my children and there was no way I was going to abandon them. By this time, I had lived alone for over 26 years. I was terrified of men and had never had so much as a date after my second husband discarded me. People often asked me, "Why are you still single?" and I answered, "Because I never found a guy that I liked who liked me."

The truth was that, when I look back, many men flirted with me in a variety of ways, but it wasn't until many, many years after my move to California that anyone of them struck a responsive chord. I believe I was gun shy and didn't want to ever risk getting hurt again. Still I have always said that no one has come on to me for fifty years but now that I think about it, several men became part of my life. I just always thought of them as a joke.

So, there I was in Redwood City evicted from my little house without enough money to pay the upfront rental deposit, not to mention the monthly rent, when a letter from Merrill

Lynch arrived in the mail. From the day I got out of NIH, I had opened a money market fund with them that earned daily compound interest. They had followed me throughout my travels, sending me statements that were so complicated I never really understood what they meant.

This time Merrill Lynch had cleaned up their act and I looked in amazement at the amount of money I had accumulated for the past fifteen years, earning daily compound interest: $40,000. In 1982, that was a lot of money. The first thing I thought when I read that statement was, *you could have paid to go to a movie.* And that is just what I did. I went to the Park Theatre in Menlo Park and when the cashier asked me if I wanted a senior discount I said, "No. I want to pay the full price."

That money was enough for a generous down payment on a house. It was enough to finally replenish my ragged underwear. And it was all mine. I could hardly believe that I had accumulated so much money. But I had.

I called a few real estate agents and told them about the money I had and the problem I faced finding a place to live. Most of them explained that with my monthly income being so low, I could not possibly get a loan for a house but two or three took me out to look at places. And then I discovered a man named David who was involved in share-housing. In the eighties, there were many young couples who earned huge salaries and could afford to make large payments on a mortgage, but they did not have enough savings for a down payment. I had the opposite situation. I had plenty for a down payment but keeping up the monthly payments would be a problem.

I loved David. He had a wicked sense of humor and we had such great fun looking at properties that I did not mind how long the process was taking. Eventually, we found the perfect home for me. It was in College Park in Palo Alto, just behind Stanford University. It was a one-bedroom place with a garage, and I loved it. David managed to talk his own brother into becoming my investment partner. The idea was that he would pay the mortgage for five years and then I would either buy him out (an impossibility) or we would sell the house and I would recoup my deposit. It was a tiny place and the asking price was $120,000.

We offered $97,000, it was accepted, and everything was going smoothly when the bank insisted that because of my actual income, I needed someone to co-sign for me. The truth was that I had forgotten that I was still tied to my family back in Toledo. I had had four years free of them, and it was the most healing time of my life. I had just begun to have faith in my own powers of survival, and I no longer felt submerged in the penumbra of their disapproval.

And now this: If I wanted a home, I had to go back to my father and beg for help.

I looked at my little puppies and my three cats and I knew I had to shelve my pride. Six little lives depended on me. We were about to be thrown into the street because my landlord didn't care that I paid him rent every month. He had sent me an eviction notice almost a year ago, and I was still in his residence. The sheriff had sent me an eviction notice not long before I got the Merrill Lynch statement. I had no more options.

I called my father.

What I did not know was that my mother had been dying of cancer for the past five years. No one told me, and I will always be grateful to them for keeping the news from me. I was the unmarried daughter, and I would have felt obligated to leave my California paradise and care for a woman I didn't like. My sister was now divorced but still living in Toledo. My parents and her ex-husband supported her, and from what I could gather, she did nothing much.

I was very wrong. She was a mother to three children, and now that I was gone, she had to run all my parents' errands, do their shopping and gardening….all the things I had done for them. And worse, she was the one who had to help my father deal with my mother's cancer. My mother had insisted that she did not want to ever be in a hospital, and my father honored that wish. He kept her at home with round-the-clock care until she died. My sister was the one who had to take her to doctor's appointments and deal with my father's needs. She was the one who was there. I will always be grateful that I escaped that responsibility.

My relationship with my mother was turbulent and soul-wrenching. She was not a bad person, although I thought she was. She believed I had wasted my life because I had all the opportunities she never had and still lived in poverty without a husband. I did stupid, useless things like read books and paint pictures. To her, that was tantamount to living like a beggar on the street. My three college degrees seemed like a waste of time and money to her. They had not given me employment or found me a husband. She believed my ineptitude was the reason my degrees had not propelled me into earning a decent living. I still could not afford a designer dress. Far worse, I did not go to the beauty shop once a week and try to do something about my very plain, unornamented appearance.

So it was that my mother and I battled each other every day we lived together, and in every fight, my mother was the winner. She never stopped reminding me of the burden I was to her from the day I was born, and the guilt I bore was almost too much to bear. I was convinced my mother knew nothing and cared less about my frustrated dreams or the wrenching ache in my heart. Now that I am older, I realize she did indeed realize my pain. She showed it each time she bought me a gift.

I have always loved music, all kinds of music. In its wordless rhythms, I found solace for tears always ready to spill from my eyes. I will never forget the Christmas I came downstairs, and there at the fireplace was a portable phonograph I could take to my room to play all the records I bought with every penny of my allowance. There, I could pretend I was the paper dolly someone loved and lost. I could believe I was the Juliet that Romeo died for.

My mother, whose words whipped me into submission, whose very glance reminded me of how useless I was, that woman I thought so cruel and unfeeling, realized that every little girl needs something that sweeps her out of herself into a lovely melody. She knew.

That year, I gave her a small stuffed bear I had made in Home Economics. It was white felt, and I had stitched it with red thread in painstaking, even stitches. I sewed in tiny brown eyes and the smile I never dared to offer my angry mother. She opened this gift that had taken me hours and hours to create and threw it in the trash. I was crushed, and even the joy of having my own source of music was soured by the way she disposed of the gift I had labored so long to create.

The next year was even harder for both of us. I hated coming home after school, and I despised being me because she had convinced me I was worthless. That year I was pretty sure I would get nothing at all for Christmas because I hadn't hidden my fury at the prison that she had made for me. She was my enemy, and I told her so every time she refused to let me sleep at my friend's house or go to a party. I screamed at her as shrilly as she did at me when she made me come home early from a dance or insisted that I didn't deserve a new dress.

That holiday, I trudged downstairs with a gift I had made in spite of myself. Deep in my heart, I could not believe that in reality my mother did not care for me. Even deeper in my own heart, there was a love for her that was smothered by the protective armor I needed to survive her attacks. I handed her a black pincushion with a lace edge to it. I had not spent the time I spent on the little bear. Why bother? She wouldn't notice anyway.

She thrust my gift aside and pointed to the present she had for me. I barely hid my disappointment. I was sixteen years old and my mother gave me a life-sized doll. I was too old for such foolish playthings, and I was devastated. I dragged the doll upstairs, and when I put her on my bed, she looked so real, I felt she could actually speak to me. I realized then why my mother had given me so juvenile a gift.

I had very few friends because she would not allow me to invite anyone over to our house after school. She and I never had a conversation. We only fought. My father ignored me, and my sister took great pleasure in baiting me against my mother. There was no one to listen to the immense inner turmoil that almost choked me; no one to care that I dreamed of becoming a great writer; no one I could tell about my loneliness, my aching need to become a valuable person.

My mother sensed my desperate need, and she filled it. She gave me a doll to talk to. I named her Penny, and I ran up to my room after every quarrel, every success and every failure, and told that doll my secrets. I look back on my high school years, and I am convinced that it was the release I felt after confiding in my silent little friend that kept me from turning to liquor or drugs to ease the terrible pain of those teenage years.

My mother and I gradually came to tolerate one another. It was only after she died that I realized how very many other gifts she had given this child she could not love. It was because of my mother that I got my college education. My father believed educating girls was a waste of time. My mother stood by me through my divorce because she knew how killing it is to live in a relationship that doesn't work.

Once I was an adult, I accepted that I had no bond with the woman who bore me. I was certain she didn't consider my moving to the other side of the country a loss to her. For me, that move to California began my life.

When I asked my father to co-sign for a house, I knew nothing about my mother's illness. Once I found out, I realized and understood why I was never notified. My mother was ill, and when you are ill, your defenses are down. She did not want me at her bedside any more than I wanted to be there. However, that is not what my father told me after that first humiliating phone call. Instead, he said, "I have always wanted a house in California. I will help you buy one, and then you won't have to sell it in five years. You can live in it forever."

I like to think his decision to help me out was propelled by my mother, but I suspect his reason went deeper than that. Daddy believed that everyone needed to have the security of a home of his own. He had just finished making a will where he set aside a trust fund for each of my sister's three children so they could buy a house when they came of age. I am pretty sure he felt guilty that he provided for them but had not done that for me. After all, I was not around until that phone call reminded him that he had another daughter.

My next year in Redwood City was filled with house hunting for a larger place with more than one bedroom. Each time I found a home I thought was ideal, my father decided it was too expensive and I would go out looking again. What I did not realise was that my mother was getting worse. My father paid for her care for six years without insurance because he had been denied due to his own medical difficulties. Each time I found a house, he had just been faced with an increase in his own expenditures, and he told me it was too expensive. But he still did not tell me my mother was dying.

Meanwhile, I was afraid I could not put off the Redwood City sheriff much longer. I simply did not know what to do or where to turn. That was when one of the women I ushered with at the Opera House came to my rescue. Julia had a yarn shop in Pacifica, a tiny community fifteen miles south of San Francisco. She also sold real estate and when she heard I was looking for a house, she said, "Pacifica is the best-kept secret in the Bay Area, never too hot never too cold, twenty minutes from downtown San Francisco and on the ocean. You would love it there."

She was right. The minute I saw what a lovely, peaceful community Pacifica was, I knew it would be heaven to live there. Julia showed me several houses, and we found one in the Linda Mar development that was good enough but not great. It was selling for $120,000, but we bid $97,000. Again, my father approved and co-signed with me.

It is illegal for banks to discriminate because of age in California, but my father was 77 years old and we were asking for a thirty-year mortgage. The bank hemmed and hawed and finally the sellers gave up and withdrew the offer. The next day, the bank approved the loan. Julia had the money for a down payment but no house. That afternoon, a woman came into her yarn shop and said, "Well, we finally decided to sell the house."

Julia said, "How much are you asking?"

"$97,000," she said.

"Don't list it," said Julia. "I have a buyer."

She called me and told me to get in the car and drive to Brighton Road in Pacifica. I did. The house was exactly the one I had in my dreams, with a fireplace, sliding glass doors to a big back yard, a large enough kitchen to eat in; and it was walking distance to the beach. I made the offer; it was accepted, and the man next door offered to do the minor adjustments to make it livable for me and my furry family.

I moved into my very own house April 1985, and I entered heaven. I honestly believe that was the step that gave me the confidence to make an independent, fulfilling life as a single woman. From the moment I entered that lovely island of peace and security, I flourished. I have never stopped. It was the beginning of the life I live now.

Here I am sitting on my very own front porch and loving that it is mine, all mine.

When Mother died, my sister sent me a box of things my mother had kept as mementos of my part in her life. I rifled through little cards I had sent to my father and pictures of me as a child. As I fingered the fragments of my mother's treasures, I paused. There, wrapped in tissue so it wouldn't soil, was the tiny felt bear I had made for her, the small token of a love I wanted so much to feel. Right under it was the little black cushion I made in my sixteenth year.

My mother seemed hard as steel to me, but she was very human after all. Yet no one bought her a phonograph so she could escape into the music she loved. No one gave her a doll to listen and accept the troubles she buried deep inside herself. She recognized my needs because they were hers. She tried to make up for what she couldn't give me in the gifts she bought for me. I will never forget that doll or the tremendous joy I felt when I played my phonograph. I took those gifts with me wherever I went, and they always consoled me. I never suspected that my mother treasured my gifts to her as much as I did those that she had given to me. I like to think that perhaps they were *her* consolation.

But, when I was fifty, the hurt was too fresh. My sister, a woman I have always considered beneath contempt, had to shoulder the responsibility of caring for both parents in their decline and, although I have very few regrets about my separation from a family that tried to destroy me, I do very much regret that I did absolutely nothing to help her out.

Six months after mother died, my father passed away. His death was instant. He had a coronary embolism while eating a hamburger and in moments, he had left this earth. My sister called and said, "Oh my God, Lynnie! We are orphans!" I am sure that this was a tragedy for her. My parents cared for her and protected her from abuse and disaster, always. They cushioned her life with money and support. She had three children they adored, and my parents provided for all four of them in their wills. I have always believed she earned every cent she got. She had to care for them for years. I did not. She had to close their estate and dispose of their possessions. I simply went on with the life I had begun to build in my own home.

For me, their death was liberation. I no longer had a family. I only had me, and I began to respect the *me* I was creating. After a while, I actually began to like myself.

A single woman alone can easily become a victim. I never realized it as strongly as I did when I became a homeowner. Two years after I moved into my wonderful house, I needed to replace the roof. The internet was just beginning to be universal and to find someone to do the job I relied on that thing of the past, the telephone book. I called several contractors and they all gave me estimates so far beyond my budget that I began to believe I would just have to live with a leaking roof. The lowest one was $10,000. My priority has always been to pay my very small mortgage and take care of my personal needs first. My pension covered that, but it gave me very little disposable income.

Jerry was a builder who lived down the street from me and befriended me because of my love of animals. He had a Golden Retriever he adored and the two of us talked dogs and puppy love whenever I walked my three past his house. I asked him if he could recommend a roofer for me that I could afford and when I told him the amount of the estimates I received. He was horrified. "You need a gravel roof," he said. "And that costs a couple hundred dollars, not thousands. You call someone and make an appointment, and I will come down to talk to them."

The man who came to give me an estimate met Jerry and they discussed what I needed. The roofer asked for $400 and did such a beautiful job that I never had to replace the roof for the rest of the 28 years I lived there.

About three years after my parents died, I decided to use the money they had left me to remodel the house. Although the place was wonderful as it was, my devotion to my art was increasing and the bedroom I used for my art studio was bursting at the seams because I had expanded to four media instead of just oils and acrylics.

Also, I had gotten in the habit of giving Saturday night potluck parties at my house. Everyone bought a covered dish and we all drank, talked, drank, sang, drank and laughed until the wee hours of the morning. At one of those events, I met an architect named Gordon, a friend of a friend I had invited. I asked him if he could help me invest what money I had from Daddy in enlarging the studio and creating a better office space. He said he was certain he could create a better space for me to work and live. He employed Niall as his assistant. The three of us drew up a workable and affordable design to remodel the house. Gordon found me a builder who gave us a shockingly low estimate. I signed the contract with him in July 1990. We arranged that the builder would complete the work during the three weeks I was in Edinburgh at its annual arts festival. At that time, I was a reviewer, not a performer, and had been attending the events there for the past two years.

I was very proud of myself. I had done all the groundwork and had not cut any corners on cost. Yet, I would have a magnificent art studio, with a framing studio in the backyard and a beautiful new front entrance to my home. I left Gordon in charge because I trusted him completely and packed my bags for Scotland.

I called him every week to see how things were progressing, but he was very vague about what was happening. When I arrived home on September 1, my house was completely gutted. There was a porta-potty in the driveway, and I could see the back fence from the front yard. The builders maintained that I had not signed a contract, only an estimate. They decided to charge me $90 an hour for each of the workers and I now owed them several thousand dollars. They would not continue the work until I paid them. Gordon could not explain why this happened. He just said he didn't know and hung up the phone.

I can still remember standing in that driveway with my suitcase at my feet wondering where I would spend the night. The dogs were in the house barking because they were hungry. The dog sitter did not come in that morning because she thought I was coming home. I drove over to the nearest motel that had a kitchen. I stood at that front desk and dissolved into tears. The motel did not take long-term residencies. I did not know where to go or what to do. The wife of the owner turned to her husband and she said, "Poppy, she is crying." He nodded and I got the room. I lived there for three months. The builder had told Gordon he would pay the motel costs because he had promised to finish on September 1, but he never did.

I could not believe what had happened. I had been so careful to follow all the rules and tick all the boxes. I stayed in that motel, cooking dinner on a hot plate and doing as much art as I could to keep from going mad. Every day, I returned to my shell of a house to walk my dogs, feed them and try to find a way to repair my home so I could move back into it. I called every consumer protection agency I could find but no one would help. There was always some technicality that kept me from qualifying for their assistance. The contractors would not resume work and I had no more money to give them. I had no idea how I would manage to pay for the motel, but the manager's wife was determined that I would be allowed to stay there for as long as I needed. I was fifty-seven, and it looked like I would be homeless.

I was looking through the phone book for real estate advisors when I saw a name I recognized. Ronnie Harris had been my boyfriend when I was sixteen and seventeen years old. He went to Stanford University as an undergraduate and it was because of his love for that school that I always wanted to go there. Now it seemed he too had moved to the west coast. He owned a large consulting and property firm that built and financed high-end buildings all over San Francisco.

I called him and told him what had happened, and he offered to mediate the situation. I didn't see where there was a need for mediation. I had signed a contract. They had reneged. Period.

I was wrong.

It took Ronnie six months of meetings, arguing, and cajoling, but he got me back in the house without further expenditure. I was still left with an unfinished house. Ronnie helped me find some honest handymen who put the place back together again, but I never really recovered from the injustice of signing an agreement and having people back out without suffering any kind of consequence. There was no way I could take them to court because I had to use what money I had left to get my home back in shape.

Had I still lived in Toledo with an uncle who was a lawyer and a family friend prominent in civic affairs, this would not have happened. An unprotected single woman with no family, no children, and no partner was an easy target. The federal and state organizations set up to protect us from cheaters and liars did me no good. I had all the proper papers and all the proof I thought I needed, but I was up against the big guys. The government agencies had me fill out reams of paperwork and then never got back to me. I was not important enough to help.

This kind of thing had happened to me before. But each time, I never saw it coming. From the time I left Toledo, I was overcharged, cheated, and underserviced whenever I tried to get help with the things that I could not manage myself. The most flagrant example was when I put an ad in the local paper to help write résumés. I was in Redwood City at the time and the dating service has stopped operation. A young woman with the worst employment record that I had ever seen came to me for help. She had never held a job for more than two months and had been fired for stealing and lying every time. I explained to her that I could not guarantee results in her employment search. I would create a résumé the way I was taught at Stanford University back in the sixties and would only charge $10 an hour for the time I spent. She agreed and paid me $30 to obfuscate her many firings and highlight what virtues she offered to a prospective employer.

A year later, right when I was tussling with the eviction notices from the landlord in Redwood City, I got a summons to go to small claims court. She was suing me because the résumé I wrote did not get her a job. I must admit I did not take the whole thing seriously. No judge in his right mind would give her the judgment (so I thought). I had never promised her a job, and her employment history was abysmal.

Again, I was wrong. She burst into tears in the courtroom and said she was alone and hungry and needed a job. I had ruined her chances of survival. The judge ruled in her favor.

Thankfully in 2002 when I was in my own home, I discovered Leo McArdle and he protected me from shysters and charlatans from then on. He babysat my dogs and he found people to do any repairs he could not do himself. It was because of him that I could pursue my comedy career, once I decided that was the direction I needed to go. He cared for the dogs when I went on the road and he was always there if I needed a ride somewhere or could not find a place I needed to get to. He still is. When I return to the Bay Area, I stay with him and his wife Carol. They are as near as I can get to a sense of family.

All the adventures I had in California, the participation in the ushering clan, the folk dancing, the freelance writing and the connections I formed with Stanford University, fortified me. I managed to write eleven novels after I moved into my house and published two of them as well as two collections of the columns I wrote for the *Pacifica Tribune*. I spent most of the nineties writing those books and trying to market them.

Then in 2000, I found a publisher. We would meet at a local coffee shop telling jokes over coffee. One day, I said, "What do you do when you have a really good book to publish but cannot find a publisher to help you out?"

And he said, "You have to know the right people. I will publish one of your books for you. Pick the one you think will sell the best."

I couldn't believe what I had heard. I had been mailing these books out for at least six years paying the postage both ways. I never got any feedback whatsoever. I assumed they were not commercially saleable books. Now I was told that all I had to do was tell this guy a good joke and he was ready to invest time and money in a book he had never read. I thought about the subjects of all the books I had written, and I believed that *Starving Hearts*, the story of my first marriage and my initial battle with anorexia and bulimia, had the most universal appeal.

He took me through the entire book publishing process, designing the book and its cover, editing for errors and gathering pre-publishing comments to put on the back cover. I learned about buying an ISBN number and about pre-arranging book talks and book signing events before the book hits the stands. The month before my book was going to go on sale, he gave me an agreement to sign that gave him all the rights for ten years. I thought "OMG I will be 78 by that time. I don't want to give away my rights for that long."

Bob was unwilling to make any changes. I refused to sign the contract.

We didn't speak again after that, and that was sad. I had loved our coffee meetings and all the laughter we shared. There had been a subtle change in the way I handled my relationships with people from the days when I was in Toledo and believed I was a victim. I finally figured out that the only one I could count on was me. I realized that friendships came and went. I had to let go of connections when they no longer were mutually satisfactory. Once I had lost the two husbands and had changed cities, I had lost any sense of permanence in my friendships. If we disagreed or if our lives prevented us from seeing one another, I went on to the next person.

I do not believe in confrontation because it never has done me much good. I also do not believe in defending myself or accusing someone else. No amount of self-justification is going to change the other person's mind. So, when I lost Bob as a buddy, I did not dwell on it. We disagreed. I never picked up the telephone to try to meet again for coffee.

It was well over a year before I saw him again and we picked up as if there had been no disagreement between us. He had left Pacifica and moved to Washington State. He had started a new life with a new woman. We chatted and reminisced, but never said a word about the book he almost published. We told a few jokes and that was it. I realized then what a kind and very reasonable man he was. He was doing me a favor and at the same time trying to protect his investment. It was a valuable lesson.

At that time, I was doing volunteer work for a woman named Janis who owned a bookstore in Pacifica. I put in endless hours there in exchange for being allowed to take books home to read and then replace on her shelves. I also conducted book talks and writing workshops. I loved being part of such an intellectual atmosphere and was more than compensated with the pleasure I got and the friends I made. The truth is that because accumulating money was so very difficult for me, I felt it was in bad taste to ask for it from someone else, especially if I liked them. I liked Janis very much.

She worked for a printer during the day to support the bookstore, which was not making very much money. When she heard about my publishing venture, she said, "I will print your book."

I was not aware that there was a difference between a publisher and a printer. Janis explained that if I gave her the galley prints, she would make a book I could sell. And she did. She printed 1,000 books for me to take out on the book signing events I had already scheduled in anticipation of a publication date. I made enough money from those books to do a second, fancier edition with my painting on the cover. That one has sold over 7,000 copies and still sells today.

I had sent a galley copy of *Starving Hearts* to my friend Ida Nissan. She was once a singing nun who played the guitar and sang inspirational jazzy songs. When I was teaching Music Appreciation at the university, I wanted my students to understand the value of all genres of music, not just the classics. I invited her to come sing for my class. That was in the 1960s. In the intervening years, she had left the convent, married an ex-priest, had a baby, and moved to Pensacola, Florida. When she read my book, she called me and said. "This book is really good. I have relatives all over this part of the south who would love to know about it. Let's do a book tour." And so, we did.

I flew to Ida's home in Pensacola and she drove me from one relative to another in Alabama, New Orleans and North Carolina, then to Boca Raton, Fort Lauderdale and other small towns in Florida. We sold lots of books and each place asked me to return. Ida and I became fast friends and we still correspond to this day. She is an inspiration to me. She started out as a deeply religious, obedient servant to her church and found the courage to defy her family and her faith, for love.

Her husband John died several years ago, and Ida still travels the world and babysits her grandchild now that her daughter is grown and happily married.

When I finally got back home from my southern journey, I was filled with hope. I was sure that I had finally found my calling. I would publish books and earn my living that way. I called the designer of *Starving Hearts* and we put together a group of my favorite columns from the *Pacifica Tribune* and called it *Thoughts While Walking the Dog*. She took pictures of me with my furry babies and we used those photos to add a bit of human interest to the stories I had chosen. I took that book with me to sell on my return to the bookstores I had visited with Ida. I also contacted both independent and chain bookstores in Northern California from San Jose to Santa Rosa. I did book talks and sold a book or two at each venue.

My biggest sale was when my wonderful friend Mildred Owen had a private signing at her home. She sat at the door with a cash box and a pile of books. No one could walk out the front door without passing her. Private book parties seemed to be the way to go if you want to make big sales.

When I traveled the country going from one Borders or Barnes and Noble bookstore to another, I never sold as many books at a sitting as I did at Mildred Owen's private party.

Lee Ann Van Der Sande and I met online because we loved Maltese dogs. She had a darling puppy named Harley and I had Dorothy, a rescue dog from the pound. I told her about my travels selling my books and she said she would be happy to arrange book signings for me in her hometown of Sheboygan, Wisconsin. I could stay with her and meet Harley.

I did talks at three bookstores but sold very few books. Then, on my way to the airport, I stopped to do a book talk at the Sheboygan Public Library. All my books were packed in my case along with my clothes and cosmetics. After the talk, every single person there wanted to buy a book. I opened my suitcase and pulled the books out nestled among my underpants, nightgowns and brassieres. My bag was a lot lighter when I repacked it and continued my journey to the airport.

I devoted most of the nineties to writing those books and selling the ones I had published. I added another Thoughts book *More Thoughts While Walking the Dog* and then after I started comedy, I decided to publish one more novel myself: *The Late Bloomer*. It was one of my favorites, and I wanted it out there just because I so loved the main character, Fanny. She was a single, tubby librarian who couldn't understand why she was not having any luck with romance. Both novels have my paintings on the cover and *Starving Hearts'* sales alone paid for the publishing cost of the other three.

In 2001, I initiated two television shows with the help of a gifted and creative producer at Channel 26, Pacifica's Public Access television station. They were a book review and arts review program called *What's Hot Between the Covers* and a hands-on art show called *Paint with Lynn*.

I produced and starred in those weekly shows for about fifteen years. The re-runs continued for another five. The *What's Hot* programs highlighted major people in the arts, and the art show usually had children doing art on camera. After I started doing comedy, I thought it would be fun to have some comedians on the program. I invited three very funny people to join me for one program and introduced it thus: "I have always told you that anyone can produce art, but today I am going to feature three people who cannot make anything worth looking at."

We all did drawings on camera, and at the end, I had each guest hold up his painting and tell me what he had learned. My wonderful friend and unbelievably talented comedian and writer Kurt Weitzmann looked into the camera with soulful eyes and said, "Today, I learned that I am a good person." That was comedy gold.

This is my beloved house.

Here I am dancing in my very own kitchen...and why not?
Photo by Vladimir Yakovlev

CHAPTER 6
Laughing at Seventy

I had been able to take Kurtis's comedy classes when I was seventy years old because I promised to write a story about them in two magazines and two newspapers and I kept my promise. This was the story I wrote:

I have spent all my life preparing for something wonderful that has yet to happen. Some people learn life's lessons in the school of hard knocks, some by example, but I sought my answers in the classroom. I managed to build enough credits for a bachelor's degree in education, drift into a master's degree in Creative Arts, disintegrate into a certificate in library science and soar to nirvana with a master's degree in communication from The Farm (Stanford University).

The year I graduated I was sure I had arrived. But I could not figure out where. Indeed, it took me a full lifespan to discover my true calling. I see me now, standing ankle-deep in a puddle of water attempting to swim while those around me splashed and spattered me with laughter. I remember glorious proms when my stockings sagged around my ankles, my strapless dress sunk to half-mast, and my date's eyebrows soared at the sight of the little I had to offer. I see myself, a three-time graduate, rushing to capture the hot story that was yesterday's headline, my hat slipping into my eyes, my pen out of ink and my subject sound asleep. Through this kaleidoscope of near-misses and almost-theres, I hear laughter, wild delighted laughter... none of it mine.

Obviously, I was put on this earth to make people laugh. Neither my professors, my parents, nor my husbands realized my gift. It took Kurtis Matthews at The San Francisco Comedy College to ignite a genius no one suspected was there. In my seventieth year, I enrolled in his Beginner Comedy Class with five comedians barely old enough to be my grandchildren. Matthews has been doing professional comedy for fourteen years and he knows a joke when he sees one. He looked me over as I entered the class and said, "You are funny!"

It must have been the purple gown and the red bonnet that tickled him. In my day, no one went into the city (San Francisco) uncapped or defrocked. My fellow students were not as careful about their toilette. They appeared, hips tattooed, tongues and noses ringed, their hips trapped in sagging jeans with see-through tops. I could see I was hopelessly out of date. While my dress hinted at what was beneath it, theirs proclaimed, "what you see is what you get" and the highest bidder takes all.

I listened to comic routines that recommended substituting Ex-Lax for Prozac to feel good, coming out in Sacramento, and choking chickens before going to work. Why had Stanford not prepared me for this kind of reality? All I learned there was how to drink beer until two a.m. and get to my eight o'clock on time.

What could I tell these sophisticated comedians that they didn't know? I rose to my feet, adjusted my girdle, shook my bra into place and it came to me! I would explain underwear! None of them wore it and they probably weren't even familiar with the term! I waxed eloquent on the advantages of a good merry widow, a solid foundation and an uplift that could change your attitude even as it destroyed your bowels.

They were amazed.

I knew then I was ready for graduate school. I studied hard, rehearsed my routines and shattered my assumptions for five weeks. My fellow students discussed blow-drying their privates and the delights of an open marriage. "He has a girlfriend and so do I," our newlywed said.

"Does that mean you have three mothers-in-law?" I asked.

"He does," she said. "I have a dog."

We all appeared at Cobb's Comedy Club for our final exam. The crowd was ready for us. They had been drinking for an hour while we all gathered in a love circle to give each other confidence. "Break a leg," they said to each other and then they smiled at me. "You'll be great!" they shouted.

"What did you say?" I asked.

My classmates got on stage and discussed issues that mattered to them. They talked about baboons in the gym, the pitfalls of balding, and the lies on package labels. Then it was my turn. "Lynn Ruth is the only member of our troupe who might die on stage," Kurtis Matthews warned.

And I did.

But the truth is I did not die. Instead, I began to live.

I could not wait to get on stage and show off. Just imagine! Thirty or forty people in a darkened room forced to listen to me! It was mind-boggling. I'd had two husbands and countless encounters with a myriad of people, and no one ever paid any attention to me at all. It was I who had to sit through their endless expositions, smile, nod and try not to yawn. Suddenly I had a place to get to in the evenings where people watched only me. I know it was only five minutes in the spotlight. But still......It had never happened for me before. I had spent seventy years fighting my way out the shadows and purely by chance, I had found a place to shine.

I had a car; I did not have a television set. There was nothing to stop me from invading the San Francisco Comedy Scene. (Except the hidden rules of that comedy scene…but I was to find that out a bit later.) For the first time in my very long life, I had a calling. And I was damn good at it. I went to one open mike after another and I never failed. Not once.

I began to notice what I wore. I began to think about makeup. I realized that if I was not to forget all my lines, I had to eat properly. I knew that I had to believe in myself to make others believe in me.

It was Tony Sparks who helped me realize I had something special to offer. He found me at 50 Mason, a club in the middle of the Tenderloin District of San Francisco, so dangerous an area that no one, with a grain of common sense, walks there at night alone.

I have never had any common sense.

I got to the club and stayed until the early hours of the morning talking to young people and learning about a world I never knew existed while I was sitting in my home writing books and painting pictures. Tony saw me there one night and came up to me afterward to tell me how talented I was. He encouraged me to do his open mike sessions at The Brainwash Laundromat and Comedy Venue, a combination Laundromat and restaurant where every comedian who has made anything of himself in the Bay Area practiced his or her craft.

Tony treated us all like stars and everyone who tries comedy in San Francisco adores him. I went to see him on Thursday nights and stayed to talk to him and love him for the good human being he is. Although he is black, he never saw that the doors that blocked his own progress had anything to do with the color of his skin. Everyone in the profession thinks he is tantamount to God because he is kind to us all. No favorites. I met with him several times to try to create a solid set, and he was encouraging and kind to me then as he still is now when I return to San Francisco for a visit.

A wonderfully enterprising woman Susan Alexander was booking 50 Mason, and she always saw something special in my performances. She booked me to do a show with Aundre the Wonder Woman, a highly educated lawyer and one of the finest comedians I have ever met in all my fifteen years on the circuit. Betsy Salkind, another sharp and enterprising comedian who moved to LA not long after this, was also on the bill. Betsy does a routine where she imitates a squirrel and spits out bits of chewed matzoth. On this particular evening, Aundre started sweeping up the crumbs after Betsy finished her set and she, a Radcliffe graduate, said, "When I think of all the years that I spent in university so I wouldn't have to pick up after white people..."

That same night Betsy took me aside and said, "A person like you trying to do comedy will have to create your own shows. People will not want to book you because of your age. They will not believe you are funny enough."

At that time, I did not realize how right she was, but six months into the game, I knew I had to create my own opportunities to perform or I would never get on stage. I was seventy-one then and it became very clear to me that people thought I was a "one trick pony" and could do a good five-minute set but no more.

I got a sour taste of that attitude about a year later. I kept trying to get paid work at Rooster T. Feathers, an established comedy venue in Mountain View, California. I had done half a dozen unpaid sets for them and I did really well at each of them. The audiences were all from Silicon Valley, most of them Stanford graduates. We talked the same language and laughed at the same social idiosyncrasies. When I asked for a proper paid booking, the booker wrote to me and said they didn't want me there. No explanation. No reason. Just no. Stop bothering us.

And I did.

I have learned that I cannot fight those pre-conceived ideas and prejudices. Betsy is right. I am too different to be swept into mainstream comedy even in London. However, I love the act of making people laugh. The process is exhilarating for me. The rejection, even the money … all that is secondary. I still get upset when I do so well with audiences and my excellent performance does not reap any rewards. I still am insulted, sixteen years later, when I dissolve a room in laughter and still am never considered for either the opening or headlining position.

However, now that I have been in this profession for a while, I realize that progression to the high-profile jobs has absolutely nothing to do with talent. I can list at least a dozen absolutely magnificent comedians whom no one has ever seen on television or read about in the papers. I can list a hundred others whom everyone knows, who have homogenized their material so completely that they make a lot of us smile and none of us laugh. They are the ones who get the bookings.

At the time I started this glorious new career, I was living fifteen miles from San Francisco in Pacifica. There were no comedy shows going on there, so I approached Don Holloway, the owner who had just acquired Winter's Bar and asked him if he would like to put on a weekly show for him. He was a very innovative and adventurous man. Although his bar was definitely not the kind that would want entertainment while they drank their beers and played pool at the table that dominated the room, he told me to give it a try.

When you are beginning comedy, it is not easy to find a place with a real audience that will give a comedian a venue to test their jokes, rather than a room filled with other comedians trying out their own material. I was able to give that opportunity to Bay Area Comedians at Winter's Bar. I started my impresario career there by creating a weekly show and then passing the bucket for donations. The slogan was, "It is free to get in, but not free to get out."

I always paid my comedians by dividing those proceeds equally among the performers. After several months, the bar began paying me a fee to run the show, which meant I could pay my performers more. However, the customers at Winter's were not interested in intellectual wordplay and social commentary. Often, when a comedian was in the middle of his set, someone playing pool would shout, "Would you shut that comedian up?"

Sam Arno, a brilliant wordsmith, once said, "If your ego is getting a bit overblown, try to do comedy at Winter's. That will get you down to size."

When Don left Pacifica and Winter's, I started doing shows at other bars in the town. Michael Slack, a master performer from San Jose said, "If Lynn Ruth ever books me in Pacifica, I just go from one bar to another until I find where she is doing her show."

I do not like competitions. Comedy is so subjective that I do not believe you can ever say one comedian is better than another….that person is just different. So it was that, against my better judgment, I entered Jon Fox's International Comedy Competition. My sweet and supportive comedy friend Mickey Joseph encouraged me to enter and because I so love Mickey, I relented. To my surprise, I got into the semifinals. I did very well and Tony, the man who created the show order for the performers, said to me, "I love booking you, Lynn Ruth. I can put you anywhere in the lineup and you will get laughs."

But when the judges tallied up the points, I was always lowest on the list. That was when I came face to face with the blocks that would keep me from progressing in this new and exciting career I had discovered so late in life. Bookers (and judges) did not believe I could sustain a laugh, even when they see for themselves that I could. I was seventy-three when I figured that out. The rejection is far subtler and even more pervasive now that I am in my eighties, but it is there. I finally have begun to realize that I cannot change prejudice as ingrained as that. I must find a way around it.

I saw then that I had to enjoy what I was doing and could not think about what bookers and club owners thought. And that love is what has kept me in this profession: I get my thrills when I get that laugh. A lot of comedians do better monetarily than I, but few get more laughs. And isn't that what all this is about?

Over the years, I have entered a series of contests. The most memorable was Bill Word's Funniest Female series. I got to the finals in that one, and then I realized that I could not compete because I had a show at the Edinburgh Festival on the date of that show in Los Angeles. "Why did you enter if you knew you wouldn't do the last show?" asked Bill.

"Because I never dreamed that I would get that far in the competition," I said.

However, the elements that made me the comedian I am today were the day-to-day open mikes and tiny gigs. I never stopped asking to be booked everywhere and anywhere. No place was too far away and most of these venues did not pay me. Once I was scheduled, I never missed a gig. How could I? It was too much fun.

In my second year of comedy a young guitar player, Ian Butler, who did musical comedy, asked me why I didn't add a few songs to my routine. "Because I cannot sing," I said.

And he said, "That makes it funnier."

"I have a song I sang at parties back in Toledo," I said. "It is Johnny Mercer's 'Strip Polka.' I used to sing it when I was eight years old…even though I had no idea what the lady was taking off."

"Let's try that one, then," Ian said. He created the musical arrangement to my song and I sang while he strummed. I put on a few layers of fancy underwear and did my first striptease in Winter's Bar. When I got down to the third layer of clothing, my accountant put a five-dollar bill in my bra. That was the first time anyone had been anywhere near that article of my clothing in at least forty years and I thought, "I am going to do this again."

In the next year or so, Ian created arrangements for me for several other songs including a parody of "Anarchy in the UK" that I changed to "I Am A Feminist." I throw a series of bras at the audience to show that I am a liberated anti-bra lady. We added Rod Stewart's "Do You Think I'm Sexy?" and I sing that after I do my modified strip even today when I sing "The Strip Polka."

I never strip to the flesh. That would not only empty the room, it would probably cause several divorces.

Soon I was being booked as much for my burlesque as my comedy. The shock of an old lady taking off clothes was so great that it brought audiences to their feet. I can still remember doing my strip in a bar in Palo Alto to screaming and shouting accolades when Jimmy Gunn, a seasoned comedian who has now sadly left this earth, said to me, "Very funny, Lynn Ruth, but always remember your bread and butter is your comedy. That is what uses your brain."

I have never forgotten his advice. I do burlesque now all over the world, but I always remember that it is the quality of my jokes that sets me apart. These days, the songs I sing are original ones. They, too, make a far stronger impression than my taking off a fancy robe and cavorting around in glittery underwear. But my bread and butter will always be the quality of my jokes.

This was the big reveal in my first strip tease performance at Winter's Bar.

CHAPTER 7
Ageing Is Amazing

I was never much of a traveler, but I discovered The Edinburgh Festival way back in the 1960s. I fell in love with the place and the ever-present frisson of creativity and excitement that permeated the place. Sadly, my lack of money and the pitfalls of life kept me from returning for way too many years. I always told myself that someday... someday, I would once again experience the electric atmosphere, the exquisite music and innovative theatre that was its hallmark.

That someday happened right after my father died. When he passed, his lawyers called to say he had left me some money. I didn't bother to ask how much. I immediately called the University of California to enroll in two of their summer programs at Oxford University studying English Literature. While I was there, I decided to spend a few days in Edinburgh at the festival before I flew back to my home in Pacifica.

The next year I decided to spend all of August at the festival. Edinburgh is a magical place both for performers and their audiences. There are endless new shows to see and opportunities to perform and hone your craft. I kept returning to see new shows and hear the exquisite classical music performed by world-renowned artists. About four years after I became a regular patron, I met Chris Cooke, the editor of *Three Weeks*, the daily review and feature newspaper for the Edinburgh fringe. Up until that time, I had always gone to the main festival events and now and again I would cram in a cheap and very funny show that was part of the fringe.

I will never forget going to see a Welsh High School performance of *My Fair Lady* for a pound (about $1.50 then). Henry Higgins was barely four feet tall and wore thick horned rimmed glasses. His trousers were buckled under his arms and his necktie reached his knees. Eliza was at least 5-foot-8 in the bloom of early adolescence. She may have towered over him in height, but he became gigantic when he sang. He had a voice that would shatter glass. The entire performance was both ludicrous and adorable. It was one of the brightest highlights of anything I ever saw at that festival since 1988 when I first returned.

Chris needed unpaid reviewers for his little paper, and he needed fast copy. If you saw a play in the evening, you had to have that review ready the next day before noon. This was before we all worked on computers. I signed up to help him out. I used to go to concerts and plays in the evening, write my review when I got home after midnight, drag myself out of bed and get coffee-ed up before 10:00 a.m. so I could walk the copy from my digs on the Dalry Road a mile and a half up one hell of a steep hill to a coffee shop on the mound (well named because it was perched high on a hill overlooking the city). I did this for several years and loved it. I got to see all the plays and concerts I wanted for nothing and to practice the journalism skills I had mastered at Stanford. What could be bad about that?

Because I was reviewing productions, I got to know the owners of the smaller venues. My favorite was C Venues. When I discovered it, Hartley Kemp created it as a tiny theatrical venue. When I discovered him, he was producing a beautiful selection of modern plays in the Overseas Club on Princes Street. Hartley is a master lighting designer for major theatres throughout the UK and he knows a good play when he reads it. I saw some of the best productions ever in that tiny theatre. My most memorable was *Eleemosynary* a play about mothers and daughters by Lee Blessing. Every now and again, Hartley would add some cabaret to his program and that was how I discovered Rosemary George and her Armenian cousin singing old-time cabaret favorites.

Hartley and I became friends after I had published my books in 2001. I was hoping he could give me some ideas on how to sell them at the festival. On an aside, I had another friend in Edinburgh who was the proprietor of The Better Beverage Company, then on Thistle Street. His name is David Halbert. He and I bonded, and when I was in Edinburgh one November I created a traditional Thanksgiving dinner at his home for him, his partner Alison, their daughter Seona. We invited Annie Kelly and Richard Ireland, both dear friends from Edinburgh. David was discussing how I could market my just-published book of short stories and he said, "Why don't you stand on the street reading from the books during the festival?"

I thought he was absolutely out of his mind, but it wasn't four years later that I was doing street performing at that festival and loving it. However, I was not selling my books. I was singing the silly songs Larry Dunlap had arranged for me to promote my comedy show.

It made complete sense that when I finished my comedy course and wanted to put on shows, the first place I thought of was the Edinburgh Fringe Festival. At that time, the Fringe Festival was THE place in the entire world for a new and hopeful artist to be discovered. Because I was a reviewer, I had no idea what the cost would be or what was involved in putting on a show. I did know that there could be no better place to polish your craft than at that festival because you performed the same show every night for thirty evenings. It was a grueling schedule but the very best way to get a production in shape.

One of my favorite comedians whom I gigged with in San Francisco was Sharman Baciagalupe (now Summers). She and I became buddies as well as fellow performers. Another was George Corrigan who was originally from England and knew how special the Edinburgh Fringe is for performers and for punters. I chatted with both of them about what they thought about coming to Scotland in August to perform and both were enthusiastic. By that time, I realized that venue costs and entrance fees were huge (and today they are out of sight). I thought if I could get several comedians to work together to make a show, we could share the costs and it would become a financially possible adventure. I called a few people I thought might be interested and so did Sharman and George.

We ended up with six people who were willing to invest time and money in the project. It was my dear friend Aundre

Herron who thought of the title of our show, *Weapons of Laugh Destruction,* and I have always been truly sad that she could not join us that summer. Several of the comedians could only stay part of the run, but Phil Johnson, a musical comedian, and I were there for the entire month. Once I had enough comedians interested, I contacted Hartley Kemp because I knew him best of all the venue producers. I wrote him and said, "How would you like some comedy from San Francisco?"

He said, "I would love that. Let's make it happen."

He thought I was bringing people like Robin Williams and Ellen DeGeneres, but of course, I was bringing rank amateurs who had never put on a show before. At that time, I was also a semi-hobby painter and was teaching workshops in Sedona, Arizona, as well as evening classes for Pacifica's adult education program. I had had a few minor exhibitions and considered myself a professional artist.

I negotiated a deal with Hartley where I did a show for him called *Paint with Lynn,* a hands-on creative hour for children during the day so that we could pay a discounted rate for our comedy show. We were scheduled to do both gigs at the old Odeon Theatre, a beautiful former movie house in Clerk Street.

Hartley had very specific rules for formatting our posters and creating our entries to be listed in the main Fringe booklet and his own brochure. I was fairly competent at any kind of writing and could send group e-mails on my computer, but the C-venue protocol was beyond me. It was Phil who made our posters and got us online with proper photos, snappy copy, and effective promotional material. We could not have done our shows without his help. He also accompanied my songs on his guitar.

I was doing the art hour for Hartley with no compensation, but he handled all the costs of entering it into the Fringe program and making proper posters and promotional materials. I knew the manager of Greyfriar's Art Shop in Edinburgh, and I convinced him to donate materials for us in exchange for a mention in the Fringe book. Hartley had long wanted to add children's shows to his listings because so often people brought their children with them for their visit to the fringe and did not know what to do with them while the adults were at a show.

Once we had our comedy show locked into the Fringe program, I tried to find lodging for all the comedians. I managed to get some of them into dormitory housing and Sharman, Julia and her partner Dallas stayed at Linton Court on the Dalry Road, where I had stayed for three of the many years I had been going to Scotland as a punter and reviewer.

The festival that year was featuring Burlesque. C Venues' public relations manager was Laura Davis, a creative and innovative publicist. When she heard that a 72-year-old woman was starring in a comedy show, she contacted me and asked if I could include a bit of burlesque. By that time, I had created my "Burlesque Theatre" routine with Ian Butler and had performed it at Winter's Bar. So, I said, "Well, I have a song I could do to end our performances," and it was settled. I would also be publicized as a burlesque performer even though I only knew one song and never ever exposed as much flesh as young ladies these days do when they are visiting Iceland in January.

I was in Sedona teaching art not long after this decision, and one of my students was telling me that what she really wanted to do with her life was design costumes. I told her about my burlesque assignment for Edinburgh and explained I needed a costume that was funny and covered up most of my body. She created a classic Victorian costume complete with a bustle, and I wear it today when I do my classic strip. It is a masterpiece.

We all worked really hard at making our comedy show a success, but novices that we were, we had no concept of what it took to have a successful run at the Edinburgh Fringe. We were competing with over 3,000 other shows fighting for an audience, and we did not do well. No one in the UK had heard of any of us. This is an international festival but most of the punters are from the UK, its former colonies and Europe. Getting an audience is the biggest challenge when you do the Fringe and it is word of mouth and all the friends you know who come there to see you that fill the house. No one in Scotland knew any of us.

In contrast, the art show took off like gangbusters. Hartley had us booked into a tiny room that first day and we could not fit all the children that came to the show into the place. I had stipulated that every child must be accompanied by an adult because I did not want to end up providing a babysitting service. Greyfriars had helped get the word out that there was a special, creative place for children of all ages. That first day we had more than thirty children each with a parent trying to take the class. There were babies in arms still breastfeeding whose mothers insisted could draw and paint. I had more children than I could handle, every age, from infants to teenagers, came to that class every day of the festival. Hartley had to move us to a large reception area in the theatre to accommodate all the youngsters eager to mess about with crayons and paper. I had a hit on my hands.

One day, an older man came into my art show with a very young child. "Is that your grandchild?" I asked.

"No," said the gentleman. "This is my son. I have him with me because I am doing a show here."

"How wonderful," I said, "What do you do?"

He said, "I am a comedian. My name is Billy Connelly."

"How lovely!" I said. "I am a comedian too and I have a show here as well. You know, if you ever want to do five or ten minutes at my comedy show, I would be happy to have you."

"That is so sweet of you," said Billy. "I will certainly keep it in mind."

I had absolutely no idea who Billy Connelly was and when I asked Laura if she had ever heard of him, she flipped. She was totally amazed that I had met such a well-known star and had the chutzpah to invite him to participate in my comedy show. She managed to get that tidbit in several papers.

It was not the art show I wanted to be the big success. I was dedicated to making our comedy show work. Because we had an hour to fill, I was open to giving other comedians a spot on our show to promote their own appearances. It was something most people who had composite shows did. That was why I invited Billy Connelly. Other performers who were doing shows did not know us, but as the days went on, I discovered other comedy shows (mostly through Laura) and after I invited those comedians to appear on my show, they reciprocated. Billy Connelly of course never did come to our show, but Inkey Jones did. Inkey was originally from Montenegro and is a self-educated, self-made comedian. He has a hearing problem and coordinated with a blind comedian named Kevin and Irish Iranian comedian Patrick Monahan to create shows in both Edinburgh and London. He performed in several of our shows, and I became one of his good friends.

The Odeon Theatre was celebrating its 75th anniversary and Laura decided it would be apropos for me to be part of that celebration. I was almost seventy-three and the oldest performer that year at the Fringe. She organized a big birthday party with a huge cardboard cake, and I burst out of that cake to sing a song. I made the front page of *The Scotsman* for that one.

Because I promised Laura to add burlesque to our comedy show in keeping with the festival theme, we ended each performance with this: "And now we have a special surprise guest from North Beach in San Francisco: Let's hear it for Queenie!" I came on the stage in my Victorian underwear covered by a flowered robe, stripping as I sang the Johnny Mercer song to Larry's backing track.

A man named Kerry Norman happened to stumble into one of these performances and after the show, he said, "I do an Oxford Cabaret Review on the Carlton Hotel at 11:00. Would you be interested in being in that performance?"

Of course, I would, and I did. Kerry's performers were all Oxford students in their final year at university. Most of them lip-synced songs and danced on stage, and I usually finished the performance with my song and striptease. Kerry and I became fast friends and since then, he has expanded from a producer to a fabulous mime performer called Kiki Lovestocking, performing and teaching workshops all over the world.

Once word got out that there was a 72-year-old comic stripper, I got invited to several composite shows and revues. Sadly, the audiences at our own comedy show were so tiny that my other performers were not happy. Sharman said, "You are performing all over the place, but all we ever do is our show, and no one comes to it."

While we were there, Sharman and I often met to write more comedy and it was she who helped me compose my signature comedy routine about dating a paraplegic that I have modified through the years and use still. It was Sharman who told me I had to get a laugh every third sentence. And that is what I still try to do.

I found heaven at that festival. I loved the people who ran the venue, and I relished all the new and exciting performance opportunities that came my way. I had an opportunity to do a comedy set every night and finish off each show with my song. I was the only one in our show who got consistent laughs from our audiences. I was beginning to think this comedy business had a future for me. I had become a minor star of the Fringe that year and I knew I had to return to perform again. My life has been a series of "almost there's" and "also rans" and now here I was stealing the limelight and seeing success within my grasp.

My comedians and I came out even at the end of the festival. No one lost money, but no one made much either. None of the others wanted to return. They had not had the rush of success I had. It was exhausting work for them, but for me, it was the first door of all those I had been pounding on all my life that finally cracked open just enough to give me hope.

When I returned to Pacifica in September 2005, after that first comedy show in Edinburgh, I was bitten by the Edinburgh performance bug and I was determined to perform there again. However, the comedy show was less than a success, although we all worked very hard at making it a profitable enterprise. I had been writing a column called "Thoughts While Walking the Dog" for the *Pacifica Tribune* and a Bay Area Director named Lennon Smith was especially fond of those stories. Right after I returned from Scotland, Lennon said, "I love your writing. Have you ever thought of putting some of those stories on stage?"

"I wouldn't know where to begin," I said.

"I can help you with that."

All that fall into the winter, Lennon and I worked on putting together a compilation of ten of my stories into a staged production called *Farewell to the Tooth Fairy*. Lennon is a superb director. I had never been on a theatre stage before, but with her guidance and her amazing patience, we did a wonderful show that we presented for two nights at The Pacifica Spindrift Theatre. It was a hit.

After Lennon and I did our show, I wrote Hartley and asked if I could do a storytelling show instead of comedy the next year. I would continue the *Paint with Lynn* show gratis. He said yes. It must be said that Hartley has always been especially kind and tolerant of my wildly extravagant dreams and total lack of understanding of what it takes to make them happen since the day I met him. Goodness and respect for creativity are endemic to his nature. He was more than willing to help me put on a storytelling show even though he had never seen any kind of outline or description of what I planned to do. The truth is that until Lennon helped me put the show together, I didn't know what I would do, either.

However, this time I had to do the whole enterprise myself. No Phil to do all the technical computer designs. No other comedians to help pay the fees and do the publicity. Hartley put me in touch with people to design my posters and help me list my shows. I paid full price for both the venue and the fringe entries. It cost me, in 2006, more than $10,000, and I made about $5,000 back. I knew I couldn't sustain that kind of expense, but I also knew I needed to return to that festival to perform. I did return the next year and Hartley helped me cut my costs considerably. I did a second storytelling show, *An Audience with Lynn Ruth Miller,* and continued doing open spots at both burlesque and comedy shows throughout all of August.

At this point, I was building a fan base. I was not aware of it, but several people looked for my name in the Fringe book that lists all the shows. The problem was they were loving my stories and not my comedy, and my true mission was perfecting my comedic skills. I did not want to lose sight of my main chance, but at the same time, I did not want to ignore the success I was experiencing with the storytelling shows. A reviewer named Julian Goodman came to my show and loved it. He reviewed for *The Jewish Star* in Edinburgh, but his reviews appeared after the festival was over. That meant that although they were very rewarding and positive, they did me no good during the festival. Meanwhile, when I was not performing, I was reviewing as well. I sensed that if I just kept at what I was doing I would find the road I needed to be on. I knew that road began in Edinburgh.

I also knew that if I did not find a cheaper way to do this, I would have to stop these yearly jaunts to Scotland. Hartley has since told me all I had to do was ask him to waive the fees, but I never had the courage to do a thing like that. I realized that if I continued to spend outlandish sums of money for my August adventure, I would have to give up my house and that was unthinkable. I began my search for a cheaper way to accomplish what I so wanted to do. I knew deep inside me that this was the way of life I needed to pursue. For the first time in well over seventy years, I woke up each day filled with excitement about the day and the week ahead. My head was bursting with joke ideas, story ideas, art projects and TV show plans. I was a happy purposeful single woman.

My storytelling show was a five-star production in Edinburgh. Because of its appeal, I made two of my closest friends I still love and see today: Fiona York who does the most beautiful rendition of *Rose*, a play by Martin Sherman, and Julian Goodman.

I did a third storytelling show: *The Other Side of the Mirror*. At each festival I attended. I also did open comedy and burlesque sets and gradually established myself as a working, viable comedian in the United Kingdom.

It was the fourth year that I worked with a beautiful human being named Patti Lockard, and we created my prize-winning musical *Ageing Is Amazing* a cabaret of parodies and original songs linked together with silly stories about an old lady who just became the entertainment director at her old age home. It won Editor's choice at *Three Weeks* that year. The show went to Brighton for its festival that next May and won *Star of Brighton*. I have taken this show to Rome where it got a standing ovation and done it several times in San Francisco. I even did it in Manila again to a standing ovation.

Here I am finally getting to perform in the magnificent Spiegeltent. What an honor.

I had found my calling. I had become a real performer. I had the potential to be a star. But I was not ready yet to do a solo comedy show on my own. It takes years to become a truly polished comedic performer. If you are really good, you can find your voice and your comfort zone in less than seven years but most of the comedians I know who are established and reliably funny to a wide variety of audiences have been doing it for a minimum of ten years and most for twenty. In my career, I have only bombed twice, but even today, sixteen years into the game, I never know if the audience is going to go wild or just sit and smile respectfully at an old lady making a fool of herself.

It was a huge challenge to keep all this going. The Fringe Festival is a money-making proposition. Landlords triple their prices; restaurants do the same; all transportation costs more than double; venues know that performers are so eager to show off what they think are their amazing talents that they will pay anything to get on stage. Publicists cannot wait to pounce on innocent artists who truly believe that all they need is one human being to see them to send them to Broadway or London's West End.

No one wants to give anyone anything for nothing. I understood that. But I needed next to nothing deals or I would have to stop running across the ocean every August to feed my ego and be a performer. My first attempt to reduce costs in Edinburgh was with a man named Peter who ran the initial Free Fringe venues. The minute I met him, we clashed. I introduced myself and said, "I have a beautiful show for you."

He said, "In England, we find it in very bad taste go sing our own praises like that."

And I said, "What was I supposed to say? 'I have a lousy show I want to do at your fringe?'"

I went home and began searching for other possibilities to accomplish my dreams. That was when I discovered Alex Petty and his Laughing Horse Free Fringe. Alex was originally a banker and then he met Peter and together they began the Free Fringe concept. However, Alex soon broke off from PBH's business model and started his own free fringe group he called The Laughing Horse. That was the one I joined, and it solved most of my financial concerns.

Alex does not screen the shows that apply to him. However, he does have favored people who have been with him a long time. He gives them priority choices for both venues and performance time slots. He finds bars and restaurants that have meeting rooms to donate space during the festival because they will make their money on the drinks and food that they sell to the people who go to those shows. British people cannot seem to sit for an hour without a pitcher of beer or a bottle of wine at the ready.

Alex charges a very small fee to performers to list their shows in his program. However, that is not the only base cost of performing at the festival. Each show pays to register for the Fringe. In addition, each performer is responsible for his own publicity and that means hiring a publicist or sitting at the computer for hours and hours contacting all the newspapers, the reviewers, and the promoters who come to the Fringe to discover talent. The actors for every production must do flyering to let people know about their show and most of them hire people to help them give out these flyers because there are literally millions of people wandering the streets of Edinburgh during festival time.

When you work for Alex's free fringe, he provides an adequate sound system and schedules you into a slot. Alex made it affordable for me to perform at that festival. I could not have done it otherwise. We all believe in our productions and, all too often, we forget that we are part of a team. When I did Alex's shows, the show before me almost always overran its time and the one after me walked into my show to set up for theirs before I was finished, to the dismay of whatever audience I could attract. The average attendance for most Fringe shows is about five. I was lucky to get that many for most of my performances and I did not want anyone spoiling the finish of my show. After all, word of mouth was (and still is) the best publicity.

Alex is a delightful and very kind man and I enjoyed working with him. However, he isn't a policeman and he should not have to be. I did not like that other acts regularly cut into my own show time.

I loved his business plan for several reasons. All the performances are free entry, but we pass a bucket at the end to collect donations from the audience. We stand at the door at the end of each show with a bucket and collected donations from what we hoped was a happy, satisfied audience.

I have spent most of my life longing to be able to afford special entertainment or treats I do not really need. It was a privilege for me to be able to let people who were in financial circumstances like mine have access to good entertainment. I was always very careful not to insist that anyone put money in the basket and I never did any hype when the show ended to try to get the audience to pay more than they planned.

However, that is an innocent view. Anyone who comes to Edinburgh and pays those bloated accommodation prices and increased food prices and a fee for a show they attend at one of the major venues can afford to drop a few coins into a basket for an hour's entertainment. Most of the performers who do free shows spend a good five minutes at the end of their show talking about how much everyone should put in the basket. In addition, they have someone other than themselves standing at the door to collect so no one gets out without having an empty basket thrust into their faces. I had no one to get to that door from the stage before most of the people exited. And I did not want to make poor people who could not afford standard ticket prices feel guilty. Very often I would end up with very little in the bucket and sometimes nothing at all.

Each year that I attended the festival, I received more opportunities to do open mike shows both for burlesque and comedy. I was on several panel shows, and a lot of the major compilation shows at the bigger venues. One of my most memorable moments was at The Assembly Rooms, with Mikelangelo and Paul Zennon hosting a performance during which a selected performer sat on a bed with the two of them and discussed their performance and why they decided to do it at the festival. I did my strip routine for them and then joined them on the bed for the rest of the show. It was the highlight of that particular August for me. A couple of years later I saw Paul in Brighton and he said, "Remember me? We were in bed together?"

I did not recognize him. I was eighty-two years old by that time and was fairly sure I had had no dalliance of any kind in quite a while. Then I remembered that marvelous experience at the Assembly rooms.

That first year with Alex. I did my shows alone with no help, but that was the year I won The Three Weeks Editor's Choice for my cabaret show and five-star reviews for both my storytelling show and my cabaret. Alex put me in the Argyle Bar, and I did a storytelling show and my new cabaret *Ageing Is Amazing*. It was there I met Susie Lochiel.

Susie was working at the time for Capital Radio, and she and her friend Laura were determined to get people to notice me. They were unbelievably helpful. I spent a weekend in London with them and they made me a show reel to send to promoters to publicize my talents and got me an interview on the radio. Susie wrote reviews of my shows and has kept in touch with me consistently since then. I consider her integral to my progress in the entertainment field in London. She has always not only come to all my shows but spread the word about them to people who matter. She invited me to her wedding in Glasgow and now she lives a short bus ride away from me in London.

It is these kinds of connections that have paved the way for my ascent in the entertainment world in the UK. You do not make progress alone; it is the people whose hearts you touch who propel you forward. The people who have helped me along are closer to me now than any family ever was. They are the bonds that keep me in London.

The second year I worked for the Free Fringe, Alex put me at The Counting House, which is a super venue for shows because it has an immense walk-in trade. Marie Woods and her husband Paul from Dublin came to the storytelling show and Marie said, "We belong to an Artist's Club that would love to hear those stories." And I said, "I would love to come to Dublin to tell them. Let us keep in touch."

That was 2007 and it took me until 2008 to manage to lock in a date with the Woods, but I finally did, and I have performed in Dublin twice a year doing both stories and comedy ever since.

It was also in 2006 that I discovered Fred Anderson. He is the key to all my successes from that point on. Fred is a street performer and a magician. He is from San Francisco and had been doing the Fringe for years before we met. He put on shows and he did street performing to earn money. It was he who suggested I get one of those granny carts to haul all my props around Edinburgh. Before that, I looked like an exhausted bag lady as I tried to maneuver down the street carrying five or six bags filled to bursting with costumes, props, makeup, schedule books and all the paraphernalia associated with creating a polished production.

Fred also kept in touch with me during the rest of the year back in San Francisco after we returned from Edinburgh. He booked me at his weekly shows at the Shelton Theatre on Geary Street in San Francisco and he scheduled me into his variety shows in Edinburgh. He loved my comedy, but he also loved my stories. I used to tell a story about the day my aunt vacuumed up her canary to end his shows at The Zoo Venue in Edinburgh to great applause. It was Fred who thought of the title *Ageing Is Amazing* for my prize-winning cabaret.. He was the one who gave me advice on ways to get audiences, how to do shows, what I needed to accomplish as a career comedian and how to withstand the stress and myriad of rejections we all get. If I am an accomplished performer now, I have Fred Anderson to thank for what I have become.

In 2009 when I was at the Counting House, I met Richard Daniels. He was exploring the idea of doing videography and offered to video my second cabaret *Alzheimer's, Alzheimer's Cha, Cha, Cha* for me. I decided to expand my UK performances and schedule performances at The Brighton Festival the following May. Richard wrote me in December, telling me he had edited the tape he had made of *Alzheimer's* and would I like to see it and re-edit it before I went to Brighton in May? He would be happy to drive me to Brighton. Richard met me at the airport and I stayed the night with him and his wife, Anne. I remember how shocked I was when I saw his home in Gerard's Cross. It looked unfinished and the living room was filled with unopened boxes. "How long have you lived here?" I asked and he said, "More than thirty years."

Anne had just had a kidney transplant that saved her life and her story fascinated me. Both of them were naturists (nudists) and I was terrified one of them would appear in the altogether. But they do not do that kind of thing, they only run around naked when they are alone or at naturist gatherings or so I gather. They were absolutely lovely hosts. After dinner, we all went to a meeting of other people who had kidney transplants in their county. When I looked at the dozen or so people gathered there, all of modest means, I realized that had they lived in the United States, most of these people would have died because they could not afford the kind of care and medication they got free in England.

The next day, Richard and I drove to Brighton and he agreed to tape my show there if I paid for his accommodation. I can still remember my friend Sarah's shock when I told her I was paying for him to tape another show when I hadn't liked the first one. Alex Petty, too, was upset. "I can get you a zillion people to tape it for nothing," he said.

However, Richard had been really nice to me and it felt fair to hire him and pay him for any further taping he did for me. It turned out this was the wisest decision I have ever made.

I had a very wise and helpful friend, Shelley Bridgeman who was only doing a three-day run at that festival. She said, "I stay with a woman who charges me nothing. She just likes the company. I will get her to give Richard my room when I am gone. How long will he stay?"

He stayed a week and taped *Ageing Is Amazing* at The Quadrant in Brighton. To my amazement, the show won *The Latest Award Star of Brighton* even though I had only been there a week and had gone home before the judges met to decide on the winner. My friend Melita Dennet, who is a journalist and a reviewer, called me to tell me I had won, and I said, "But it wasn't that good."

She said, "Never say that. Just say thank you."

That August, Richard drove me to Edinburgh and, to my surprise, he decided to help me out doing all the things I had tried to do very inadequately myself. The truth is that it was he who made the shows I did at the Free Fringe such a success. He helped usher the people into the show and he was there to collect the money when they left. I never hired him, and he never said he would help. He was just there at every show for me. I have never understood what made him do it, and I have never stopped being grateful that he did.

I employed another very young man who called himself Digory for technical help that year. He was a student from Glasgow and I grew very fond of him. Richard did all the extra things that other performer's partners or friends did for them. It was only because of him that I made money at the after-show collections. Now, I had someone making sure people got to their seats before I began my show. I had never had anyone to help me with those seemingly small but very vital tasks before. When he left after two weeks, I missed his help and I missed him. He became and still is a great and understanding friend.

Each year now, I was doing at least two shows at both the Brighton and Edinburgh Festivals and appearing in at least three others every day. It was a heady time for me. I have always considered myself a failure; someone who just wasn't good enough to be great. Yet, when I walked down the street in Edinburgh, everybody seemed to know who I was. August and May became the highlights of every year for me and cemented me into this career that I discovered so late in life.

In May of 2010, I met Bill Smith, who owned The Latest Music Bar in Brighton. He also owned a magazine that was a theatre review vehicle that combined theatre features and reviews of real estate listings. At the time we met, he was in the midst of planning to open Brighton's first public access television station. He came to a performance of *Ageing Is Amazing* the year before and that year he watched *80! A Cabaret*. After he saw both shows, he said, "Why don't you take the best numbers from each of your shows and put them together into one big smash hit with a band and some visuals?" and I said, "Because I do not have the money to do anything like that."

"I will produce it for you," he said.

I was amazed, flattered and thrilled. It felt like an offer from heaven. I should have remembered that old saying, "If something seems to be too good to be true, it isn't."

Bill and I made plans for me to return to Brighton two weeks before I went to Edinburgh and begin our work on this composite production. However, in early July I broke my heel and had to have surgery or I would never walk again.

I was devastated. This one festival that held so much promise would be the first one I missed in all those I had attended since 1988. Bill was really lovely about the injury. He called me several times and promised that we would resume work the next April before I came to Brighton. At that time, I was also working with Vladimir Yakovlev on a coffee table book he was producing called *The Age of Happiness*. He came to my home early in 2010 to interview me and was very taken by my humor and my views on life. Most of the elderly people he interviewed for his book were doing physical feats that older people do not even want to do, but I was creating shows and expanding my mind.

Vladimir invited me to do a show in Moscow for him and we set the date for the end of October in 2011. Since I had broken my foot, I had lost two big chances I would never get again, all because I fell off a ladder. This was my third great opportunity and I was determined to make it happen.

And indeed I did.

I managed to get well enough to go to Moscow by October. He had stayed in touch with me and encouraged me during my recuperation. He told me he wanted me to write a book about ageing, and I began it, but soon discovered the slant he wanted was not what I was giving him. I have my own writing style, and it was not his. The good thing that came out of the project was that it absorbed me and gave me something important to do so that I did not dwell on what I had lost by missing the festival and not having a larger show produced that was supposed to be my very first smash hit.

That October when I went to Moscow, I was finally able to wear high heels on my swollen foot. Vladimir paid all my expenses and put me in a boutique hotel that was very French. It even had a resident lovebird. It was a magnificent experience and one I have never duplicated. I had never stayed in a five-star hotel before. I had never had anyone pay my expenses for the gigs I managed to do. I had never had anyone give me a guide to watch over me or take me to lavish and exciting restaurants to experience different ethnic delicacies. Vladimir made me feel like the star I never dreamed I could ever be.

He provided me with two translators to help with my comedy show and they were interesting, very well-informed people. I asked them why Putin kept getting re-elected when everyone knew he was a dictator and a crook and they said, "You see all the wealth and sophistication that is in Moscow and you do not see the extreme poverty and sense of desperation in the country and the smaller cities. The peasants believe their only chance to survive is with Putin at the helm. And they don't care what methods he uses to give them that security."

However, the day Vladimir scheduled the show was the day the entire world pushed its clocks back an hour to return to standard time. Putin decided that Russia would stay on daylight savings time another week. So, although everyone's computer recorded the time as an hour earlier, the nation did not. No one in Moscow knew what time it really was or what time the event was supposed to begin. To complicate the confusion, the night before there was a huge snowstorm. Transportation was blocked for much of that day. As a result, there were very few people in the audience.

Vladimir was a wonderful host, and I was squired from one place to another, eating beautiful meals, meeting marvelously intelligent people and trying new foods. Vladimir introduced me to a local brand of Slivovitz so strong I thought my insides would combust. As we left the restaurant, after I had tasted this 300-proof drink, I could barely stand up. Still a bit bleary-eyed and tipsy, I saw a display of giant teddy bears and pointed to a large white one. "I want one of those," I said, and before I knew it, I had it in my arms. I took my new bear to my hotel room and had to leave half my things in Moscow to get it in the suitcase. I named him Mischa. That last weekend in October 2011 was amazing and erased my bitter disappointment that I had lost my big chance in Edinburgh.

Meanwhile, Bill and I were making plans to create a show to put on in May at The Latest Music Bar. Bill is one of the most creative, impractical men I have ever met. His ideas are expansive and inspiring, but he has no idea what it costs in manpower, money, and time to produce them. His sidekick and former wife is the one who makes all his dreams and plans happen. However, she was not happy with spending a lot of money on our project and our plans never materialized.

When I returned to Brighton in April to create the show with Bill, his mother became very ill and he left Brighton to be with her in Wales. He gave the job of putting this new show together to Val, an enthusiastic young lady originally from Israel. Val has very extreme and innovative ideas, but sadly they are too out of the mainstream for me. I tried to go along with her vision because I liked her and respected her judgment. The problem was with me. I simply could not imagine being made up so grotesquely or pretending I was a senior slut. My moral base is locked into the forties and fifties. I am a nice Jewish girl. No way would I bare any flesh below my shoulders. No way would I intimate that I was a hot sexy bimbo because I am not that at all. I do not even know how to be one. I do not believe in women making the first move. I only have sex with men I marry. I thought a blow job was filling balloons for a children's party. In my mind, the back door is in the kitchen. In short, I am a prude.

I am not an accomplished singer, dancer, or actress. I just have stories to tell and an irresistible urge to share them on stage. Val did her best to spice up my presentations, but what we finally ended up with was a disjointed show using most of my own parodies and three of Bill's songs, with projections that had absolutely nothing to do with the storyline I was presenting on stage. We did the show for the Brighton Fringe and for the Brighton Lights Awards Ceremony. It was well received, but it was not a winner and I did not feel confident about it. It felt incomplete and fragmented to me.

The plan was to take the show to Edinburgh to perform in the fringe festival; Bill would pay for the venue, a pianist, and all production costs as well as a place for me to stay. Alas, Bill decided to pull out of the deal in July. However, since he had already paid a lot of money for the venue, he told me I could do the show but it would have to be on my own. He would not pay for any production costs or lodging, and I would have to do the entire production without a pianist.

I was crestfallen. I had missed the festival the year before because of my broken heel. I had been dreaming of this unique opportunity to showcase my beautiful shows with all the things I could never afford: costuming, expensive props, technical help, videos…and now I had a venue and a show that needed music and visuals and expensive production with no way to make that happen. I had received no pay for the months I spent in Brighton; I had exhausted my pension funds. What to do?

That was when I called Richard Daniels. I knew I could not possibly pull off a show with projections and technical demands that were beyond me. However, Bill had paid for a slot at Hartley's C Venues. I did not know what to do to get this show I had been working on back up and running, and I was desperate not to lose all the effort I had put into creating it. Richard said, "This is your eightieth birthday year, and you are going to Edinburgh. I will take care of this."

He called Bill and together they formed a workable plan. Richard did all the technical work involved with the show including projecting the videos and running the sound system.

He had to make several trips to Brighton to arrange for all the equipment he needed. Bill would pay for our lodging. Neither of us would be paid for our work. I remember waiting for the money promised me to cover our expenses and I was sure Bill would renege at the last moment. He did not. He gave me the money when he drove me to the station to catch the train to London to meet Richard.

It was a miracle of negotiation that got us through that month. Richard drove me and all the equipment up to Edinburgh. We stayed with Margaret Santandreu, a very good friend of mine who gave us a reduced rental. She gave us each our own room and we still had money left for food for the two of us for a month in a city that doubles its prices in August and is dedicated to overcharging performers for everything.

Staying with Margaret had its ups and downs. The first night there, C Venues had scheduled our tech rehearsal for midnight. It took a good four hours to go through the videos and sound cues. When we finished, we realized we had no key to the flat. Margaret was fast asleep, and we could not get into our rooms. It is cold and not very summery in Edinburgh in August, but to my amusement and Richard 's fury, we were stuck in his car until 7:00 the next morning. That would not have been a tragedy except that we both had to be bright and sharp to do the initial preview of the show at 6:00 p.m. that day.

I was not happy with the videos Bill and Val had created for my show. The production itself seemed to lack the kind of sparkle I had always infused into my cabarets. We named it

Granny's Gone Wild, after its signature song, one Bill had composed. There was very little learning for me to do since most of the songs and patter were taken from my previous shows. The problem was that the show was boring.

The first two performing days of the Fringe Festival are preview days and my talented, clever friend, Sarah-Louise Young, who is an accomplished cabaret performer, came to see the initial production. She sat down with Richard and me after the show and made several suggestions to tighten up the script and alter the videos. Richard got out his camera and we created two new videos and got rid of the ones that were detrimental to the plot of the show. I worked on deleting and adding bits to the script to clarify what we were trying to say.

That month became a heaven for me. Each performance of *Granny's Gone Wild* got better and better. Richard and I established a beautiful rhythm to our days. He was always awake before I was, doing his video work. When I got up, we planned the day and rationed out the money we had from what Bill had paid us for food. Then we went our separate ways and met up at various points during the day until we performed the show. Our teamwork was as near as I had ever had to a relationship. It was hard work, and it was great fun.

Karen Rosie helped us with publicity and promotion. I had discovered Karen when I did shows for Funny Women and she agreed to be part of our production effort. We three together were an efficient and very effective team. By the second week, we all felt the show had legs. We did not get huge audiences, but we did get wonderful reviews and we were very proud of the result of all our work. The final version of the show was very different from the one Val and Bill sent up to Edinburgh. That original one didn't work. This one did.

Richard and his wife work at a beer festival the last week in August every year, so Karen took over the technical problems for us the last week. We had lots of help too from the C Venues staff. The show seemed to have a strong impact on its audiences and got a great positive response. Then, at the beginning of the third week, Frodo McDaniels, who was on a panel to find the best cabaret of the Fringe, called me. I was shortlisted for the Best Cabaret of the Edinburgh Fringe Festival Award. I could not believe it, especially when I saw the other wonderful shows I was competing with.

I won it.

Even now, six years later, I cannot believe that I got that prize. It is so sad to me that Richard, who did most of the work to make the show flow properly, was not there to accept the award with me, but Karen was. It was a memorable moment, among many in my life, but it still shines above the rest. I can remember my shock when they called my name. I have seen so many others win awards, and they are always so gracious and poised. It is thrilling to watch them accept their prize and thank all those who helped make it happen.

Not me. They said my name and I completely fell apart, crying so much that no one could understand a word I was saying. I forgot to thank everyone. I almost forgot who I was. But I did remember to tell that audience that if they have a dream they should go for it no matter how impossible it seems.

The prize was a two-week run of the show at London's Soho theatre, all expenses paid. I would receive a performer's fee and so would my pianist. I chose Robert Pettigrew to play for me because he is the musical genius who composed all the songs for my show *Approaching 80* (later to become *80! A Cabaret*) and I wanted him to get some of the recognition he so deserves. We had several of his songs in the show, which made it all the more appropriate that he be at the keyboard.

When Bill realized the show had received such a huge honor, he immediately took possession of it and said he was due the money we made from the ticket sales at Soho as well as an extra fee paid to him as a producer. All this seemed so wrong to me. He had paid for the venue and Richard's and my board for the month. He received all the revenue from the ticket sales at the Fringe for that investment. He also received all the revenue from the initial performances we did in Brighton. But we had put in an immense amount of work to repair that initial production. We had redesigned the show and made it work. Surely our time was equal to Bill's monetary investment.

Still, the show would never have happened without Bill Smith. It would never have won anything without Richard and Karen (or me for that matter), and we all deserved some compensation for the time and sweat and tears we poured into that production. It was Richard and Karen (certainly not me) who managed to forge a proper deal with Bill that gave all of us money, not just Bill. He received filming rights to use for his TV station. He got proper credit for his part in the production, but we were paid the money awarded to us. The show was to go live on stage in April 2015.

I was finally recognized for the time and effort I had spent investing in both festivals, Edinburgh and Brighton. I was now an established performer on the London scene.

Me jumping out of the birthday cake.

CHAPTER 8
Overcoming Fear

People wonder how I can gather enough courage to get up on stage and speak to a bunch of total strangers. That is a minor challenge compared to the ones I faced from the day I was old enough to take stock of my environment. I realized then that I was living with an angry mother who blamed me for being stuck in a marriage she never wanted in the first place.

When I forgot to put my hand in my lap when I ate, or interrupted her when she was screaming at Daddy, "I have had enough of you, Lynn Ruth. You almost killed me when I gave birth to you and you have never stopped driving me mad."

I never knew what I was doing that I had to stop, but I knew damn well I better stop it or else. I spent most of my life being afraid of things, but I never would admit to that fear. I knew that if I did show any weakness, my mother explode. And the one thing I feared more than anything in the whole world was my mother's anger.

For most of my life I was afraid to make an independent decision. I thought I needed permission. I think that fear actually began when I was six years old, and Anita Save came over to my house to play. We decided to play beauty shop. "I'll go first," said Anita, and she cut off all my hair.

"Now it's my turn," I said.

Anita said, "No, it is dinner time. I have to go home."

Just then, I heard my mother's car pull into the driveway and I said, "Uh-oh. If my mother catches you here and sees what you did to my hair, she will kill us both. We better hide."

Anita pointed to a large cupboard next to the bed. "Let's go in there," she said.

We both crawled into the cupboard and shut the door, but we didn't realize that that there were no doorknobs on the inside of the cupboard. We were locked in. "If we yell, will your mother kill us?" Anita asked.

"Yes, she will," I said. "She might not kill you because your mother would get angry, but she will definitely murder me."

Anita started to cry. "I don't want her to hurt you," she said, "But I am really hungry. It is dinnertime."

"OK," I said. "Maybe you can talk her into just sending me back to the Indians."

We pounded on the door until my mother found us and although she was very nice to Anita and even gave her a hankie to dry her tears, she did not bother to hide her fury at me. She turned to me and said, "You look disgusting, and it serves you right. That's what you get for making decisions without asking me first."

"Are you going to send me back to the Indians?" I asked.

My mother said, "No, I am not! You are so ugly now that even the Indians wouldn't want you."

Well, time passed. My hair grew in, and I wasn't sent to the Indians, but I never lost that sense that I was incapable of making a decision. That is why something as simple as finding an address or cooking a roast terrifies me. I am certain I'll forget the butter or take the wrong turn or end up with no hair on my head.

Everyone is afraid of the wrong things, not just me. I wallowed in fear until I was well into my fifties. Bit by bit, I learned to ignore the doubts that stopped me and get on with my life. I still have not eliminated fear and that is a good thing. Every adventure, every decision has pitfalls and the trick is to recognize them, allow for them and continue to move forward.

When I think of the young frightened child I was, the terrified teenager and the uncertain adult that was me, I realize that all that energy I spent in avoiding my blue devils could have been spent in so much more constructive, positive explorations of what life can give to us all. The difference between me then and now is that I do not let my doubts stop me.

It is amazing to me how much I learned from my mother. She was smothered by her insecurities and she molded her life to avoid facing her fears. I saw how unhappy she was, but I was too much her victim to feel compassion for her until after she was gone.

It is so sad to me to remember my mother sitting in her spacious, beautifully decorated house, huddled over the TV set watching born-again Christians preach sermons because she was so afraid of death, she thought these television ministers could save her. She hoped they would pave her way to a heaven she never had on earth.

It breaks my heart now to remember her alone in that huge house afraid to go outside unless her two sisters were with her or my father took her with him. She descended so far into herself that all she could think about was her body and her premonition that she was going to die before my father did. She was so determined to get cancer that, when she finally did, I realized it was the only wish my mother had in her whole life that actually came true. That to me is a human tragedy.

I watched my mother descend into her black cloud of despair and I knew that I could easily do the same thing if I allowed it to happen. But because she allowed me to go to university, that opened my eyes to a bigger world. Thanks to that I was able to step outside my terrors and get a grip on life. When I taught school, I would stop the children from cheating by saying, "I don't want you to be like the one on your left or the one on your right. We already have one of those. Be like you. That is what the world needs."

I follow my own advice now. I am proud to be me. It is, after all, the only thing I have to give to the world, and I know that when I leave, it will be a better, richer place because I was in it.

I think the big tuning point for me was when I moved into my own house. I was 52 years old. Somehow, knowing that the place I lived in was really mine gave me unexpected courage. What I did not expect is that my neighbors were very aware of the way I lived. I am not a morning person and because I have not had a regular job to go to since I was 36, I tend to keep irregular hours. It did not occur to me that this would offend the people who lived on my street. After all, I was in my own house living my own life.

I know now that others who live a different lifestyle intimidate people. Because so many of my activities are late at night, I have always slept late in the mornings and eaten my final meal after I get home from whatever gig I am doing. The rhythm of my life makes me unavailable for people if they like to do early morning appointments. I still cannot understand why that makes others angry to see that I have not shriveled up into a non-functioning ball just because I do not get out of bed until well after 10:00 a.m.

I am all too aware that single woman alone is a vulnerable target. I have seen that kind or inequality play out every time I am evicted from a flat for no real reason or given half the salary I expected for twice the work. People think they can manipulate a woman alone and force her into patterns they believe are more acceptable. It is disconcerting for others to see someone prospering without the restrictions they have set for themselves. Society has taught us that two-by-two is the way we need to live to be happy. When people see I am content and motivated in my life, it seems to infuriate them. The older I get, the more apparent this penchant to either be ignored or overlooked becomes obvious.

I have been the target of unexpected and unexplainable rage for most of my single life, but until I got into my own house, I never had the courage to fight back. Instead, I obeyed the demands of my oppressor.

Diane lived next door to me. I particularly liked her three children and they often came over to visit me. Her son Kevin was a special favorite of mine. He was about fifteen years old when I moved into my house. I will never forget his coming to my house that first New Year's Eve after I moved in, and asking me "What is sex like, Lynn Ruth?"

I had no children of my own, and I had never been given "the talk" by my mother. She let the school take over that responsibility. In addition, my own experience with an angry, demanding husband who smacked me around and a gay one who couldn't stand the sight of me didn't really equip me for explaining the psychological and physical ins and outs (literally) of sexual intercourse. However, I needed to say something to this boy who thought he would shock me by asking such an uncomfortable question. I told him what I believed but had never experienced. I said, "Sex is a physical satisfaction… anyone can do it. But it is enhanced and enlarged when there is affection and respect. You can sleep with many women, Kevin, and it will soon become the same old, same old. But if the two of you have an emotional and intellectual bond, it will become something new and exciting every time you are together."

Instead of getting a confusing answer that would amuse him, Kevin heard something that made him re-evaluate who he was and what he was feeling, and so we bonded. He often came over to me for advice and sometimes when his mother set up barriers to keep him home and under her wing, I would solve it by lending him my car or letting him use me as his excuse for being away from home. What I did not realize was that Diane resented this friendship and began to resent me for encouraging it. It all came to a head when her daughter Kelly offered to clean my house. After she left my house, I realized I was missing a coat I had in my closet that had one of my mother's brooches on it.

I discovered the missing coat the next morning on my way to Scottsdale, Arizona, for an art workshop. At first, it didn't occur to me that Kelly had stolen the coat. Why should she? It was neither her style nor her size. When I called her home to ask if she had seen the coat, her father shouted abuse at me. I hung up the phone, confused and uncertain. I had not accused his daughter of anything, and I still did not absorb that the girl had deliberately taken the coat. Within five minutes, Mark, the youngest son, came over with the missing coat... minus the brooch.

When I returned from Scottsdale, I went next door to retrieve the brooch. I assumed it had fallen off the coat The pin was one of the few things I had from my mother, and it was quite valuable. However, whenever I knocked on her door, Diane was always sleeping or unavailable.

Now, I became angry. That was a memento from my past, and I wanted it. I obviously wasn't going to retrieve it peacefully. Before I had moved into my own house, I would have simply accepted that I was a victim again. This time I determined to get back what was mine. I reported the loss to the insurance company and to the police.

I will never be convinced that I did a wise thing, but I know it was the first step in speaking out for myself. I paid for that report for the rest of the time I lived in my house. Diane reported me to the animal control authority for having more than one dog, a regulation no one in Pacifica has ever even noticed. When Kevin graduated from high school, I gave him a bottle of champagne. Diane reported me for giving an illegal substance to a minor. When I did some renovating on the house, she called the local building inspector every day. He said, "Why are you calling me? She has proper permits for everything she is doing."

She apparently said, "Eventually she will break a rule, and I am going to catch her at it."

And so, I lived with a next-door neighbor determined to get me arrested, but instead of running away and hiding, or changing my behavior, I was not afraid to defy her. I continued adding dogs to my family. I finished the building project. I was slowly realizing that one person objecting to you was not a flaw in *my* character. It was a defect in hers.

My confidence grew the longer I stayed in my own place. I can still remember when a friend's wife decided I had posted a remark online that was detrimental to her husband. She barged into my house and began screaming at me. Instead of dissolving into tears or flooding her with excessive apologies as I always had with my mother, I said, "I do not tolerate that kind of behavior in my house. You are trespassing on my property. Get out." I reached for the telephone and she left. This was a very rare occurrence for me. I had won.

This determination to stand up for what I believe in became stronger as I aged and perhaps that is why I felt very little fear when I got on stage for that "final examination" at Cobb's Comedy Club. I knew I had a right to be on that stage, even though I certainly did not fit the demographic of the class. It never occurred to me that people my age did not get up and tell blue jokes. When I told my jokes, everyone laughed. Isn't that the point?

As I became immersed in the San Francisco comedy scene, I realized that many of the people who run comedy venues do not pay their performers. Their reasoning is that they are giving people stage time and without stage time, you cannot develop your comedy set. However, these bookers are charging admission and the bar is selling drinks. A group of people is giving them a show, and someone is making money from it.

Surely the people creating the event deserve to be compensated.

When I first began doing open mics, I did not expect to be paid, but I saw many young and very capable comedians on the bill with me, who did not have a pension to live on as I do, allowing themselves to be exploited. They were so brainwashed by this unfair system that they didn't have the courage to stand up for themselves. They began to feel that their talent had no value. My first act of rebellion against that practise was at my own comedy shows at Winter's Bar when I paid the comedians from the bucket collection.

However, I continued to do my own performances for other comedy clubs without expecting any monetary compensation. And then I went to a marketing workshop in Austin, Texas. I had performed an original song at their Burlesque Festival and won awards both nights. I stumbled into burlesque and I thought it might be interesting to learn the nuts and bolts of that kind of performance.

Burlesque demands huge expense in costume and dance lessons, directing and choreography. Comedy does not. It only costs in transportation and in time. At that burlesque workshop in Austin, the leader said, "If you do a performance without demanding payment, you are depriving the rest of us who have invested thousands in our art from getting a paying job. Why should a booker pay someone when he can get equal quality for nothing?"

And the penny dropped.

I was a novelty performer in comedy and in burlesque. I was good at what I did. If someone could get me in their lineup for nothing, why should they book someone who demanded fair pay? I vowed never to do that to the others I worked with ever again.

Not long after that, I was booked by John, a promoter in Pleasanton, California, for a Friday night performance. Friday night is the worst commute of the week in the Bay Area and Pleasanton is a good sixty miles from Pacifica. During the middle of the day it will take about an hour to get there, but during rush hour, it takes as long as three hours. I was not being paid for that performance even though John charged admission to his shows. I called him the beginning of that week and asked if he would give me gas and bridge money to do his show. I fully expected him to say fine, since that cost to me would be at least $40 and I was doing his show for nothing.

Instead, and he was absolutely furious with me. He insisted that I had no right to ask for money for the privilege of being in his prestigious lineup. I thought if all of us who do his show would insist on payment, he would have to compensate us or not have a show. Someone had to make the first move. And I decided that someone was me. I canceled the gig.

I doubt very much if that changed John's policy, but it made me realize that if I wanted to advance to a professional status, I had to demand payment for the work I do. I need to do that for my own self-esteem, and I need to do it for all the others who relied on their comedy to earn them a living. This all came to a head when I was asked to do an all-women's weekend of programming in San Francisco.

The small theatre for that show has something like a twenty-person capacity, but it is great fun to do and we all support it because its owner donates most of the money earned there to end worldwide female genital mutilation. When I was asked if I would headline the show, I was told we would each receive $20 per performance. There would be two performances each night. I promised to help book the show, and I promised each woman who accepted that she would receive $40 for the evening.

However, the first night, after I finished the evening, I was informed that I would only receive $20 for both shows, not for each one. Furthermore, I was only being paid because I was the headliner. I replied that I would return the next night only if I was paid and if the producer paid the other women. I confirmed my demand with an email. When I arrived that Saturday, I asked once again if all of us would be paid. I was told that would not happen. The other performers were sitting in the room and heard my request that they get the pay they were promised.

I said, "Well then, thank you very much, but I am not performing tonight." I expected the other four women to follow me out, but not one of them moved. I was shocked. I made that stand for them (and for me, of course), and not one of them stepped up to the plate.

I have carried this battle for comedians to be treated fairly with me to the United Kingdom. The comedy field there is glutted. There are so many comedians that bookers can book people for pennies and for nothing just for the prestige of doing a show. I will have none of it and lose lots of gigs because of it. There is a series called Funny Fecklers that is well respected and gets nice audiences. However, they do not pay their comedians, and they do charge admission. When I was booked for that show, I asked what my pay would be and was told that there is no compensation. I said, "I will do this if nothing else comes along, but what you are doing is very unprofessional."

"Well then," the booker said, "Then don't do it."

So, I didn't.

And of course, he was right. We all know the terms. We all have the right to say no. But in my mind, unless more of us say no, the practice will continue, and comedians will be exploited as long as standup comedy exists. I am not alone in this fight. Actors Equity in the UK has formed a special comedian section and that group fights for those of us who are promised money and never receive it. However, they don't do a very good job of protecting the lesser names on the list. It took me months to get them to send a letter to a man who promised me money and simply ignored the obligation. One booker deducted a substantial booking fee from my payment without telling me in advance. I complained to Equity, but nothing changed. What was worse, even though I sent emails proving that the charge was unexpected, the gentleman at Equity said that the booker had said I was lying and he believed her. So the truth is that Equity only protects the people they feel are important enough to shield. And often those people are already well-established performers making enough money to absorb their losses. I am not there…yet

On the other hand, that organization has helped me advertise my shows in their newsletters, which is an amazing help. They have launched a very active militant campaign to ensure that women are paid equally to men. We need to begin somewhere, and I firmly believe Equity membership is that good beginning. I am aware however that I am not a big enough fish to warrant individual help.

That is why I love Angel Comedy in London. It is run by comedians for comedians. Barry Ferns got the idea to form this unique club and together with a group of other comedians, renovated an older building in Islington they named THE BILL MURRAY and created a nightly comedy show there and at another venue within walking distance, the Camden Head Bar. They operate on a shoestring, but they pay every one of us who perform for them. The entry is free, so their houses are packed. They pass a basket after each show and hopefully what they get covers their costs, although I doubt it.

I am very proud to be part of their organization because places like that can help restore the self-respect that all performers deserve. They have expanded to giving pay-as-you-wish comedy courses and allowing us to put on our one-person, hour-long shows there, receiving all the profit except for a small fee that goes to them for doing all the ticketing and front-of-house duties. They are restoring the pride we all take in our work because their shows are always excellent, and we are all paid for our time and talent. To me, that is how it should be.

People have told me over and over again that I am fearless. They are right. I am. Now. You cannot intimidate me. I am not afraid to say what I think, and I am well aware of the consequences. I am willing to suffer lost gigs and lost payments to be able to look in the mirror and know I have done what I think is right. I could not have done that as little as ten years ago.

But I can now.

Here I am in my brand new re-modeled kitchen playing the ukelele for Louise. Photo by Vladimir Yakovlev

CHAPTER 9
Funny Business

It never occurred to me that I would ever stand before a group of strangers, microphone in hand, telling jokes. Of all the professions that interested me, standup comedy was certainly not on the list. I intended to be a wife, and a mother, and when that didn't work out, I wanted to become a primary teacher, a professor, a novelist, a journalist, a columnist and a reviewer. When I was seventy years old, I stumbled on that comedy course. One crazy thing led to another and the next thing I knew I was on stage telling jokes to audiences not just in San Francisco but more importantly on the Edinburgh Fringe.

When I attended those comedy classes, I never realized that standup comedy is a business. I thought it was an idle pastime for fun. I never knew people did this kind of thing for a living. In the beginning, when I was doing open mics, I didn't see anyone who was memorable enough to think this was an art that had to be cultivated over time. I thought it was something people did just to get a laugh. No other motive.

After I started meeting with Tony Sparks to discuss how I told my jokes and what jokes to tell, I began to understand the challenges of creating comedy that appeals to many people rather than a specific few. Mike Moto, a very capable comedian from San Francisco says, "The art of comedy is to get a lot of strangers to come to the same conclusion that you have come to." He means that you must get people from a diverse potpourri of backgrounds to laugh at your joke. You need to strike a universal chord.

Everyone is afraid of ageing. No one wants to do it. Yet the alternative is *really* unpleasant. That meant that my very presence gave people hope that they didn't have to fall apart at the seams, sit at home locked to a TV screen, popping a plethora of medications so they could survive. It is my very presence that shows my audiences that the way you age is a choice. That means that before I say a word, I have an advantage over the other comedians in the lineup. Everyone wants to believe that anyone who is over seventy can have a social life, even if the result is a total disaster. For example, I say, "Sometimes I get lonely. That is why I read the obituaries for romantic leads." That is funny. But they think I am really doing it, that I am looking for romance when I am so past the accepted dating age that it becomes ludicrous. And in the back of everyone's mind, they are thinking, "Yeah. When I am seventy-five, I'm going to go out on dates, too. Just like she does."

I suspect it was that first experience in 2005 at C Venues that locked me into a comedy career. I did not know that standup comedy was a young man's bailiwick…indeed I did not know standup comedy was a cultivated, polished art until I started doing it. I did not realize that women were not welcome. I did not know that the older you are, the less chance you have of getting bookings. What I did know was that I could make people of every age, from sixteen to sixty, laugh. Of all the careers I tried, this one was the only one that gave me a rush of satisfaction, a moment of glory and the feeling of success every time I did it.

It was victory that hooked me. It is still amazing to me that some of my biggest fans are young girls. Some men don't relate to my comedy until they are in their thirties and forties. The thrill of communicating across the generations is intoxicating to me, and despite the battle I have convincing bookers in major clubs to notice me, I know that my audiences always laugh when I get on stage. They love me because I love them.

You need to be thick skinned to do comedy. You need to accept that some jokes won't work, and you need to take responsibility for their failure. I have learned that it is *never* the audience that is causing the silence that every comedian dreads. It is my delivery, my timing, the quality of my humor. If they aren't laughing out there, I am doing something wrong. I have heard too many comedians tell me they had a bad night, the audience was the wrong kind, the stage wasn't properly lit. None of this is true. The one thing I have learned is that funny *is always funny*.

The older you are, however, the harder it is to get into the big clubs. There is a trio of men in their mid-fifties who cannot get booked at San Francisco's major comedy club because of their age. I was told by a booker in Silicon Valley who heard her audience scream and clap for me that I was not professional enough for her audience. The answer to that kind of shortsightedness is to go where they *do* accept you and make your own gigs if you can.

Although I find that I personally do not "get" a lot of the jokes younger comedians tell, I know when they haven't done their job. I can hear it in the audience's reaction. If something is stated correctly, has an element of surprise and is told professionally, it will get a laugh. It makes no difference if the comedian is male or female, old or young. Comedy is an art, and only 10% of it depends on the actual words you say, 90% is *how* you say what you say and the way you connect with your audience.

This is the never-ending challenge...one that still interests me after sixteen years. I like to think I get better every time I take the mike. I get sharper and my jokes work better the more I do them. I am not there yet...not by a long shot. Standup comedy is an on-going process and that is its fascination. No matter how successful you think you are, there is always room to get better. My goal is to get people to laugh so hard they need to change their underwear every time I am up on stage. I cannot count the number of times an audience member will tell me "I want to be you when I get old," and their praise is exactly why I love getting on stage to tell my jokes.

Comedy bookers do not go to many shows. They look at videos of performers and they think about what will make their audiences laugh and what will look good on their website or the posters they put up to advertise their events. Old women do not sell comedy tickets and a promoter's job is to sell seats.

That is why all women, young or old, perform under a smothering penumbra of pre-conceived notions. The powers that be do not think women are funny on stage. When they see a woman getting billows of laughter, they think "That is a one-off. She will never be able to keep that up for a forty-five-minute set." Worse, when they see an older woman take the stage, the first thing they think is, "I wonder if she will last through her set?" And then when I do a solid half hour of jokes, they will shrug their shoulders and say, "Those jokes are predictable. They are all about being old." Which is what I am. Comedians talk about who they are and what is happening in their lives. I am old. That is what I talk about.

The hardest thing for me to swallow is that talent and the ability to make people laugh has nothing to do with climbing the comedy success ladder. I first experienced that when I tried out for my first paid comedy gig at The Punchline, a famous club in San Francisco. That club is where many professional comedians do their stuff. There is often a headliner from out of town, but the host and the feature are local people who are well-paid for their time. Comedians that play there have made it on the San Francisco comedy scene. Comics such as Robin Williams, Ellen DeGeneres, Rosie O'Donnell, Drew Carey, Chris Rock, and Dana Carvey took their first comedic steps on that stage. Tom Rhodes plays there regularly and so did Will Durst.

The booker wields immense power because that club is the ultimate goal of every Bay Area person who wants standup as a career. There are no other choices there. Local comedians nearing sixty are not headline material, so magnificent comedians like Johnny Steele, Larry Bubbles Brown and Michael Meehan have formed their own night called "The Dinosaurs of Comedy." They have a midweek show, never a weekend.

I tried out successfully for that club. The booker would not have even let me try out if it hadn't been for another very well respected comedian, Kurt Weitzmann. He was the one who talked her into letting me try out on stage before an audience. The night I did my audition, Amy Schumer was headlining. When I finished my set, Amy told the booker, "That woman is funny."

We took several photos together. Now she is a huge name in comedy, and when she came to London to perform at Top Secret Comedy Club, she remembered me. Once again we were in the same show together. It was only because of her that I was booked on the lowest rung of the comedy ladder. In the United States that is the MC.

I am not a particularly good MC. You need to banter with the audience to warm them up and my hearing is not what it should be. I miss the answers to the questions I ask, and my responses make no sense. My immediate recall is not the best and the names of some of the comedians whose roots originated in third world countries defeat me. However, once I launch into my jokes, I am as good as any that have appeared on that stage.

Ageism and sexism are the elephants sitting in every comedy club and they pop up continually for me. In Sacramento, I was scheduled for a Thursday to Sunday run and my job was to open the show and introduce the comedians. Fortunately for me, the manager there really liked me and my work. However, the headliner was upset that a senior woman was on the bill. When I returned to the club on Friday, he said, "You know, after you do your opening, you can leave, and we can each introduce each other. That is a very long drive late at night for someone your age."

I informed him that I could manage the drive but I heard later that he also complained to the booker. Luckily for me, the manager of the club defended me and I completed the fou-night run.

I did get to perform with a national headliner, who some call the Prince of Pain. We were at Cobb's Comedy Club, also owned by the people who own The Punchline. I was really delighted for this unexpected opportunity to be at Cobb's, a much larger, more famous comedy club. When I got there on Thursday, I was handed a list of do's and dont's when dealing with our famous headliner, who was a very egotistical, demanding man. We were not allowed to use any four-letter words in our sets. We were not allowed to drink in front of him. We were not allowed to use the green room because he needed privacy. And then, for me alone: "The star does not want you to introduce him. He does not want you on the stage before him. Introduce our feature and then get off the stage."

When this man got on stage, his set was peppered with pornographic references and words so blue even I would not say them. He made a point of talking to Nato Green, the comedian who featured, and avoiding me. I have always thought of myself as thick-skinned and able to handle negative situations. However, each day when I was relegated to a back table, I could feel my stress level rise. I never realized how upset I was or how closely connected the mind is to the body until the Saturday night performance. I woke up that morning with a cold and cough so severe I could not speak. My voice was gone, and my nose was dripping like a broken fountain. However, I made a pact with myself long ago, when I got out of that protracted hospital stay at NIH that truncated my activities for more years than I like to admit. After I walked out of that hospital I said, "That is it. That is the last time your body is going to call the shots."

I was thirty-seven when I made that resolution and I have never broken it. Which is why, sniffling, sneezing and wheezing, I got into my car that night and drove to Cobb's. I did my introductory set, listened to a national comedian who had no respect for others blast his obscenities into the microphone. On Sunday, the day after the performance, my "cold" disappeared.

However, the worst insult to my ego was yet to come. In August of the year I moved to Brighton in the UK, I heard that Tom Rhodes was performing at The Punchline in the late fall. Tom is a very good friend of mine and a very kind man. I wrote him and asked if he would find out if I could feature for him and he did. I got the gig and flew to San Francisco the morning of the Thursday I was to perform. All my friends who heard I was returning flocked to the comedy club to hear me and to say hello. I decided since so many people would be in the audience who had heard my comedy before, I would do some of the longer stories that were so successful for me in the UK.

I got into San Francisco at 4:00 p.m. and had to get to the show by 7:30. My jet lag was immense, but I had decided when I signed up to do this kind of performing that I must somehow not let that fatigue and inability to focus my thoughts interfere with my commitment to perform. I managed to get to the club, and since I was a featured act, I had a 20- to 25-minute set. I got up on stage and rocked the house. The next night, I was rested and in much better shape. The manager came up to me before the show and said, "Tom Rhodes has asked to be able to do a longer set, so we are cutting your set in-half. You will do ten minutes for the rest of the run."

This is unheard of in comedy protocol. I have sat through dozens of feature acts that did not get any audience response and no one ever cuts their time. If they cannot do a decent job, they are simply not hired again. When the week was over, I asked Tom if he had requested more time, and he said no, he hadn't.

It all goes back to the attitude of the industry itself. It does not believe women are funny. Period. I would guess I have done a minimum of 4,000 gigs in the fifteen years I have been going on stage, and I can count on one hand the number of times there has been more than one woman on the bill. It is no different in the UK. Women must be twice as good to get half as far in the industry and old women do not exist. This is the battle I fight wherever I go.

Old, young, male, female or both, we all have a tough road to follow in comedy. The competition is immense. There are easily a couple thousand comedians working the UK circuit alone. Getting noticed is as difficult as if you were a needle in a haystack of eager, pushy, ambitious performers.

The truth is that there is no instant success. You must make the calls, do the follow-ups, get on stage as often as you possibly can. You need to always listen to the audience. You owe them that laugh. Hecklers are hecklers because they are either bored or drunk. The majority of the people that come to a comedy show are people who paid to be amused. It is our job to do that. And if they do not laugh, you were not funny.

The big names in comedy make money; lots of it. The people who are on television or in movies make money at comedy as well. Those doing the circuit, slogging from one venue to another, one town to another, and in my case one country to another, are not so fortunate. That isn't why we keep doing this. Laughs are our currency. It is hard to believe that a working standup comedian will travel two hours to get to a gig, talk to the audience for ten minutes, receive a nominal fee, and then spend two more hours traveling back home without thinking twice about it. In fact, we will probably do the same thing the next day and the next.

Standup comedy is addictive. Once you get that laugh, you want another and another and another. To add to the challenge, creating good material is a catch-22 situation. You do not want to keep telling the same jokes over and over again, but you cannot determine if a joke will work until you test it out on an audience several times. The solution is to go to open mics where you are not paid. You test the jokes to see if they work. The problem with an open mike situation is that the audience is usually small and made up of other comedians who do not listen to you at all. They are too busy writing down what they are going to say. The good news is that after you have been doing comedy for many years, you get a sixth sense about what might work, and you can often sandwich a new joke between two sure-fire ones and see how it goes.

Because the competition is so intense and the field so crowded, I have begun to branch out to other countries and other continents. I am a regular on the Dublin comedy scene now. It took me almost eight years to manage it, but now I send out a few strategic e-mails and my week is booked. Here is what happened the last time.

I went to Dublin in November and did what everyone does against our better judgment. I took the cheapest flight I could find because it is travel and accommodation costs that eat up the fees you are paid. Once I got to the airport and experienced the rudeness, the long lines, the inconvenience, that is the hallmark of Ryan Air, I was contrite, and it was too late.

However, I had no time to stew. I had to get ready for my first headlining gig at Anseo. I have been headlining at this wonderful small room on Camden Street for at least four years. It is run by a prince of a man named Jonathan Hughes who has built that club up from nothing into a comedy staple on the Dublin scene. I did a forty-minute set for him and discovered that the Irish are still squeamish about some of the landmark decisions that have come down from their higher courts. I made a reference to the woman whose rapist was not convicted because she was wearing a lace thong. Either they didn't get it or didn't want to. They did love the one about all the pipes leaking in Dublin's ancient buildings. ("I can relate to that" is the punchline.) They also got the one about how my generation killed their roaches…and the young people smoke them. That one doesn't go over very well in London.

Thursday, I went out for lunch at House of Fraser's Café Zest, which is very upscale. When I asked for water, the waitress said, "Anything else?" and I said, "Yes, I would like it in a tinted glass." I was trying to be funny, but she took it so seriously that she got someone else to take care of our table. I didn't get the tinted glass. I also need to remind myself to keep my wisecracking on the stage.

Thursday night was my first night at The International Comedy Club. That venue is the reason I return. It is run by Aidan Bishop who is top of my admiration list. All comedians complain about the glass walls we need to break: the unsaid prejudice toward women, minorities, disabilities and age. Aidan gives everyone an opportunity at his club and not only that, he pays his comedians fairly. To make the experience even nicer, there is always a good audience at The International. That means everything to a performer. It is a lot easier to tell your jokes to fifty people than it is to ten no matter how badly those ten want to laugh.

When I first visited Dublin, a young lady took me past The International and told me that it was THE place for standup comedy; no other club came close. It is not that way anymore. There are several clubs that equal The International in popularity, but Aidan's club has managed to still hold its top rating despite the new competition, and I personally love performing there. It is a small room and on weekends many people must stand at the back because there are not enough chairs. There is no microphone, so we have to project our voices, which can ruin a good throat, but all of us are willing to risk laryngitis to do a set there. The crowd is always attentive and anxious to laugh. Often, there will be so many patrons, that some will be sitting on the stage.

When I do my comedy there, I always feel that this is how stand up should be done. There are enough people there to make the laughter spread and yet it feels like you are talking directly to each member of the audience. Aidan often is the MC, and he has mastered the art. He is funny and welcoming and sets the stage for us all. One of the things that really matter to every comedian is the amount of time we get to strut our stuff. Most comedians check their watches when they go on stage and time themselves. However, I am utter crap at timing, so usually whoever takes the tickets comes in and waves at me when it is time for me to stop. On this Thursday, all the comedians were involved in conversation outside the room and no one bothered to tell me I had overrun my time. Our minutes are our currency and all comedians want to stay in front of that microphone for as long as they can. It was a great night for me! I was on stage for forty minutes!

Friday night was my big night. I was booked in three comedy clubs: The International; Anseo's new Friday night show; and Comedy Gold, Emily O'Callaghan's new room. The audiences diminished as the evening progressed. I left the International (it was packed with standing room only), to get to Anseo's new Friday night where twenty people were waiting for me (the headliner) and then off to Comedy Gold where less than a dozen tired, drunk patrons were waiting to see the late-night headliner. The interesting thing about all these rooms is that I arrived ten minutes late to every one of them and I still had plenty of time to unwind before I went on stage. Evidently, Irish time is like Jewish time….absolutely unpredictable. This rarely happens in London. You almost always go on very close to the time you are scheduled. The English pay attention to time.

The Irish comedy scene is growing and very solid, yet everyone there that I talk to wants to come to London where they think the action is. I certainly felt that way in San Francisco, but now that I am in London, I wonder whether wherever you are doing whatever you do, you always think the market is more open somewhere else.

One of the things that makes my Dublin trips so marvelous is that I stay with this magic family that reminds me of an episode of *Leave it to Beaver*; a happily married couple with three amazing sons, and a tight, loving family unit with aunts, uncles, cousins, grandparents all intricately woven into their lives. When I am here, I am treated like another granny—fed, pampered, and transported to my gigs. This is an immense novelty for me, after all. I have lived a very long time and make all my arrangements, get myself to wherever I am going and make sure I am properly fed. For this short period of time, I get all the rewards of being a grandparent in a large functional family without having done any of the groundwork. I also get to play with two dogs. A tiny Jack Russell and a huge, insecure Borador (lab and border collie).

I have amassed a lot of very good friends now in Dublin. I found Linda Hayden. doing comedy at the Ha'penny Bar, a wonderful venue run by the delightful Tony Ferns. It is one of those open mikes I spoke about where every comedian goes to test out their material because Tony gets in a real audience and gives everyone a chance. He even gives a prize at the end of the show. I have won that prize several times. This was Linda's first time at doing comedy, and she was sharp as a razor. I told her so and she and her sidekick for the evening, Sue Kirk, joined me for a drink.

Since that time, I meet Linda for dinner every time I go to Dublin. In addition, she put together a tour for me in Galway. I stayed in her home and met her two dogs and her delightful niece. Now, Linda is into politics and fighting for women's rights in Ireland. She still does comedy, but her main goal in life is fighting for equality, abortion rights and proper respect for her gender. These people (and there are many more in each country I visit) have become my support group. They are always there for me when I come into town.

Saturday night, there are two shows at The International and both are always filled. This time there were two new comedians. Robbie Bonham, who is in his forties and has that wry Irish wit that always makes me double up with laughter. I am convinced that a great deal of comedic ability cannot be learned. It was Bonham's very Irish-ness that made his jokes even funnier. I know that being Jewish has always given me an edge; and black comedians usually have a dimension to their delivery that adds to every joke they tell.

As our world becomes more diverse and television and the internet reduce our differences, I suspect this will not always be so. The more we assimilate, the more we lose those special ethnic characteristics that add flavor to our jokes and our conversation. Much as I applaud universal acceptance of everyone everywhere, I think this loss of ethnic identity is a loss for us all. I know we are all alike essentially, but there are attitudes and mannerisms that are handed down generation to generation that I hate to see homogenized.

The other comedian at The International Saturday night was a Dublin native, now based in London. His humor, too, was sharp and beautifully worded. He was a difficult act to follow. But follow I did.

That intense week in Dublin convinced me that I love the performing life. It does not tire me. Instead, each show I do and each success I have inspires me to go further and do better. Is this what being professional is all about? Or is it the stuff of a nervous breakdown?

Sunday was my last performance at The International and it was wonderful. Sunday night is normally a slow night, but this night was very crowded. I was in the first section and David McSavage, who is very famous in Dublin because he is on TV, was the headliner. The interesting thing about this night was how diverse the audience was. We had a huge segment from France, so English was their second language, and a girl from Lithuania had no idea what was going on. We all managed to hit a responsive chord and the evening was a success despite the immense cultural diversity of the audience.

It is always sad to say goodbye to Dublin. The Irish have a way of taking you into their hearts, and the family I stay with makes me feel very loved and important. However, I was brought back to reality sharply when I approached Ryan Air for the return trip to London. Rules are rules, and by God, you are going to pay if you don't follow them. As I stood in line at security (this time my bag was checked, a gift from my Irish family), I saw a man who could barely speak English (and obviously did not understand the regulations) gulp down a huge bottle of tea as fast as he could. The poor fellow gurgled as he sloshed through the line and I couldn't help thinking, "How on earth would that container of tea with all the tea bags in it have endangered anyone but the poor guy who had to drink it, so he wouldn't have to pitch the container? I have seen the personnel at Ryan Air pat down a tiny baby and all I can say is I hope the kid had a giant poop as the inspector checked out his diaper.

The other interesting thing about this trip is the number of single women I met there in their late forties and fifties who are feeling unfulfilled. They are at that "is this all there is?" stage of their lives. Do men get that feeling? Or do they just go to a porn site on the computer and wank off? These women in Dublin were all earning a good living, but still feel they want more than coming home to an empty house with only a dog or a cat to greet them. There is no way I can explain to them that these are normal clouds before the rainbow splashes gorgeous color on a grey sky. It is very much like what Winston Churchill said: "When you are in hell, keep going." Middle-aged womanhood is not hell at all, but it can feel very bland. For some reason, none of us realize that the best is yet to come. But it is. It certainly has for me.

After that Dublin adventure, I went to a gig in Cannes. My French adventure was very different from the Irish one. I had never been to Cannes and was not familiar with how to get around or what the comedy scene would be. I was very excited about experiencing a new place. I knew the pay would not be great, but it was worth the effort to me.

When my plane landed the sun was shining! At first, I was alarmed and didn't know why I didn't have to turn on all the lights to see my hand in front of my face. Then I realized I was not in London, and when you are out of that city, the sun does its job. Vanessa, the woman who runs the comedy show I was about to be in, met me at the airport and her mother, who is a wild, adventurous driver, drove us to her flat. As we darted from one lane to the tree on the side of the road into the highway and across four lanes and a traffic bump, I stifled an impulse to call my friends and to say my last goodbye, but we did indeed get to Vanessa's flat intact.

Her mother served a homemade pizza which I devoured with champagne as Vanessa and I discussed the profession of comedy and the insensitivity and stupidity of her university students. She has a Ph.D. and two master's degrees, and it made me wonder why she is so devoted to talking dirty to crowds. I know *my* reason, of course, is that it brings back memories of my youth and all the things I was too afraid to try.

The hotel I booked is called The Hotel Bellevue, and it is adorable. It has fourteen rooms and a very caring concierge named Alessandro who sent me comforting messages telling me he would be sleeping when I arrived, but I could get into the hotel with a code, and my room was ready. Because Vanessa and I chatted until after midnight, I did not get to Cannes until 1:30 a.m. I sent Alessandro a message thinking he would get it the next morning, but I was wrong. He responded that night and managed to get me an extension plug for the lamp in my room and to greet me in his pajamas, which I thought was very French. And adorable.

My room was without a doubt the smallest area I have ever seen that could be called a room. A broom closet would be a better label, but this one had a double bed, a desk, an itty-bitty closet, a functioning bathroom and a balcony. It was indeed the size of a disabled toilet stall, but somehow it was very complete. All I can say is it is a good thing I am 4-foot-10 and weigh less than one hundred pounds or I would never have fit into the place. It felt like I had just entered Jonathan Swift's Lilliputian village.

Since I got into my hotel at 1:30 a.m., I didn't get to bed until 3:00. When I awoke, the breakfast time was over (even in France!), but darling Alessandro (this time in proper shirt and trousers, and still very cute) took me downstairs to make me a coffee. I was expecting real French espresso viscous as syrup but instead, I got half a teaspoon of Nescafe and a lovely smile from Alessandro. He even carried the cup to my room and fit it onto my teeny little desk with the minature red lamp and little laptop. Life was very comforting here at the Bellevue. I felt loved.

Speaking of being loved, I must say the world does indeed dote on the elderly these days. At the airport, the young man at the coffee shop washed my ecological cup and gave me a huge discount on my cappuccino. Then he tidied the table and washed the cup after I finished. A lovely Englishman from Birmingham stood behind me in the line to board Ryan Air and carried my case down the stairs without my even asking. The woman in the seat next to mine who was from Essex chatted with me the entire two hours we were on the flight. Not that I *wanted* her to chat for so long but after all, she is from Essex. What can you expect?

After Vanessa and I finished our conversation and I drank all that was left of the champagne, I called Uber to get me from Nice where Vanessa lives to Cannes where my cute hotel was located. My driver was Charlotte who took me into the hotel and opened the door to my room because I cannot work keys; I couldn't do tampons either. You get the picture.

As I said, the whole fucking world just loves the elderly except when they are doing business with them. I decided to take a walk to find a place for lunch in Cannes and it abounds with many, many eateries with menus in French. So, if it isn't a crepe or an omelet, I have no idea what it is. Finally, I found La Civett Carnot which said Brasserie and by god I may be Jewish, but I know what THAT means. The food there was all right and the service was very fast. One person there spoke English: the chef. However, if you speak only English, or you are older, or a woman, beware. I ordered a weak coffee and got charged for a double espresso. What I got looked like one shot to me but maybe the French think small when it comes to coffee. Naturally, I complained. Two very large imposing men insisted that a double is what they gave me and too bad for me. I feel certain had I been able to speak French, or had I not been a single ancient hag they would have adjusted the bill. The amount is inconsequential, but the attitude and the dishonesty are not.

My gig was called *The British Invasion* and was in an Irish bar six minutes from my hotel. However, I got confused by the little blue dot on Google maps and the six minutes expanded to thirty as I wandered the streets of Cannes searching for my destination. The comedy show was interesting and well attended. The comedians were very inexperienced, but the audience was thirsty for a laugh and the show was a success. I headlined for them and the response was gorgeous. I even got a Caesar salad, two drinks, and a bit of cash.

I managed to find my way home with the help of two escorts and it did indeed take me six minutes to get to my hotel. Which all goes to show Google does not lie. The next morning, I took a bus to the airport, got a flight to Gatwick, came home to grab my burlesque costume and took my clothes off to a standing ovation in Islington. As we all know, a girl must do what she has to do.

Me with Amy Schumer at the Punch line.

I finally became part of the Dublin comedy scene. Photo taken by Zak Milofsky.

CHAPTER 10
The Joke's On Me

I have a definite protocol before I go on stage. I always dress up. Steve Martin said, "Always dress better than they do" and I take that advice to heart. I am always very nervous before I get on stage, so I make it a point to listen carefully to the reaction that other comedians are getting and adjust my set to include what I think this particular audience prefers. I never take notes up on stage. They know I am old, and I want to prove to them that my memory is as good as the other comedians they see in the show.

The truth is that it is not. When someone says, "How do you remember all thirty minutes?" I always say, "You don't know the two hours I forgot."

If the audience does not laugh at a punch line, I always panic and speed up my delivery. It was Amy Schumer who told me "If you have said something funny, WAIT for that laugh. When you pause, they know you said something funny." I try to do that, but I do not always succeed.

The jokes a comedian tells are very funny to him. I can still remember how hard I laughed at the joke about my second husband and the bellboy as I wrote it. However, it is very important NOT to laugh when you tell your joke; that is the audience's job. They need to believe all this really happened to you.

And that is another point: Everything you say must be believable. I do a joke about horseback riding and everyone knows I would have a helluva time getting on a horse. They do not believe me until I say, *I never dreamed I could get my legs so far apart.* Now they are with me because it sounds like something that is true.

When you are on stage, you are thinking on three levels: The first is what you are saying, and it is vital that it looks like you are just chatting with the audience. The second level is what you are going to say next, and the third is how the audience is reacting. If they are silent, you need to change direction. To do that, I always stop and start asking someone in the front row a question. There are very few topics I don't have a joke about so that starts me on a new set. In this business, a senior moment is suicide.

Every word I say has been written down and that is so for most truly successful comedians. The word order is as important as the word itself. I have found time and time again that if I move words around, the joke fails. The most important thing to do when you get on stage is have a killer opening line and a solid ending. You must leave them laughing.

The next thing to remember is that the audience must like you. That means that you need to come across as a nice person. If a heckler begins to interrupt you, do not snap at him (it is always a him…a very drunk him, as a matter of fact). You simply ignore the person butting in or you, smile, and nod at him. In my case, I usually cannot make out what he is saying anyway. I have always maintained that in sixteen years I have never had a heckler, but I cannot swear to that. What I can say in all honesty is that I have never *heard* a heckler.

When I go up on stage, this is what happens when I say what I say (but not all of it all the time):

I am Lynn Ruth Miller and I am eighty-six years old. I am your future… if you're lucky. Every woman in this place is looking at me saying "No. I will NOT let myself go the way she did."

I love looking at the women in the audience and nodding because indeed this IS what they are all thinking. I often have people coming up to me and saying, "Are you *really* eighty-six? You don't look it." And I say, "Oh yes, I do. This is exactly what eighty-six looks like. If I took off my clothes, you would not doubt me."

And so, the comedy goes on. *Well, don't worry. You will look a lot better than I do… you have Botox; we only had Scotch tape. And speaking of Botox and all the alterations we do these days to our bodies: All you girls want bikini waxes. I have great news for you: If you wait long enough, you won't need one."* (If a woman nods to show she understands, I always give her a high five.)

One day you'll look down… AND IT'S GONE, and all you have is a camel toe. (If someone laughs before I get to that punch line, I usually say, "Has it happened to YOU?")

And sex is more fun. In my day, it was over in seconds; now if you can wait thirty minutes, you get four hours. Although God only knows what he will do with the extra three hours and fifty minutes. Crochet? Believe it or not, in my day, we didn't use condoms. We had babies. Welcome to my world.

I started comedy when I was seventy because I didn't want to peak too soon. I was born in Toledo, Ohio, in 1933, the worst year of the great depression. If my parents could have afforded a movie, I wouldn't be here. I was supposed to be born in August but didn't arrive until October. Whenever my mother got angry (which was all the time), she would scream, "You were always slow right from the beginning." And she was right. (Here, I always interject "Who has children?" and the response is smaller every time. Then I say to a mother, YOU will know how slow I really was.")

I didn't get teeth until I was two years old, but once I got them, I kept them all. And they are all filled with gold. And you can get good money for an ounce of gold these days. That's enough for the plot AND the casket.

I didn't walk until I was three. That means I spent a lot of time on my hands and knees... I still do; it keeps my boyfriend happy. I couldn't ride a bicycle until I was sixteen and by that time, I wasn't interested in two-wheelers. I was too busy figuring out what was going on with the birds and bees. I never got that right, either.

Flash ahead a good sixty years and a hot Sicilian named Bob was trying to come on to me. We were talking about sex because that is what hot Sicilians like to discuss best and he said, "Oh, you never forget. It's like riding a bicycle." So, I made him dinner.

In my day, the policeman was your friend. You could talk to the nice stranger and nothing happened. And when a politician shook your hand, and he didn't touch anything else. And neither did the priest. (This is the rule of three…I use it very often in my comedy because it builds a bit of suspense.)

Telephones were really boring. The only thing you could do with them was to ask an operator to dial a number. Now you can take pictures with them, search the internet, get directions. These days if I lost my fingers, I would be mute. And I would never have an orgasm.

We didn't go to doctors; we asked our mother.

When my father got his hand caught in the lawnmower, my mother said, "Serves you right," and poured a bottle of iodine on his hand. "That hurt," said my father.

"I know it did," said my mother. "That will teach you to put your fingers where they aren't wanted."

Does anyone remember cellar doors? (These days very few people know what I am talking about, but once I explain that we used them to get into the cellar without going into the house, the rest of the joke works.) *I used to love to slide down our cellar door. It was made of wood and I got dozens of slivers embedded in my backside. When that happened, you didn't go to your mother; you went to your father and he took them out with a needle. "That hurts," I said.*

My mother said, "Oh just shut your eyes and think of England."

When I got married, I was very innocent. We had a wedding night and I had no idea what was going to happen to me. I asked my mother, "What's he going to do to me?" and she said, "Oh, just shut your eyes and think of England."

"You mean he is going to give me splinters?" I asked.

"You could call it that," my mother said.

I got a catalog from Victoria's Secret today. I was shocked. That underwear is meant to be seen! It wasn't that way when I was a girl. Our underwear protected us.

My mother didn't let me out of the house without six layers of clothing under my clothing. She thought that would protect me from beer, pretzels, and testosterone.

When I was young, I was so hot that when my dates came to pick me up, they didn't ring the bell, IT did. (Here is one of those instances when I always pause. The audience always takes a moment to figure out what I mean…but they always get it, which is more than I did in those days. I was a good girl.)

Buying adult underwear was a rite of passage. Your mother took you out for lunch and told you all the other horrible things that were going to happen to you now that you were a woman. Then she took you to the corset department to buy your first brassiere.

*A woman whose name was Hazel – they were always named Hazel-*This always gets a laugh and I have no idea why – *with a chest like two bags of dog food, a mustache, and a tape measure around her neck said, "Can I help you?"*

My mother said, "I want to buy my daughter a brassiere."

She looked at me and said, "Go get your sister, honey. I need to measure her."

"No. It's me. I'm the one who needs a brassiere," I said.

She turned to my mother and said, "Why don't you bring her back when she doesn't look like a piece of plywood?"

That afternoon I bought myself a 32D bra and two bags of Styrofoam to fill it and I was ready to go out on dates.

*We used to go to drive-in theaters. Remember those?-*This is another time when I pause and ask the audience if they know what Drive in Theatres are- *If we were lucky, we didn't see the movie. It was dark in that backseat and you lost everything: your wallet, your keys, your virginity.*

Our formal wear was not like the little nothings you girls wear now that make your privates public. We concealed what we had until it was too late for him to change his mind. When we put on an evening gown, we wore a torture chamber under it invented by Rasputin who sold it to Blue Beard when he wanted to do S&M on his wives. We called it the merry widow. To wear it was to give up oxygen for the remainder of the evening. It was eighteen inches in circumference, and it took three people with strong knees to get you in it. But once you were in it, it pushed all your body fat up to your chest and you got cleavage. Let's hear it for cleavage. - And they always clap.

The problem was that when I attached it to my stockings (we did not have pantyhose). The entire contraption slid to my knees (no hips) and my dates would say, "What's the matter, Lynn Ruth? Do you have to go to the bathroom?"

So, to keep the corset up, I stuffed my bodice with my mother's expensive bath powder mitts.

The style of dancing then was to hold your date's hands and move together thus. Here I demonstrate the way we danced. *When my body collided with my date's, mushroom-shaped clouds of powder erupted from my chest and my dates always said "Gee Lynnie, you smell good!"*

And I said what we all said in the fifties, "Oh let's not talk about ME. Let's talk about YOU and what you plan to do to earn a living." Well, tonight I stand before you.

Well, tonight I stand before you barely shaking, my underwear dry. The reason I am in such good shape is that I don't do what you do all night… I sleep. And I don't have someone with a runny nose and full diaper wanting me to bake cookies and tell him I love him. I divorced him. (This is misdirection…an unexpected punch line. The audience thinks I am talking about having children.)

The real reason I am in such good shape is because of my attitude. I got that attitude from my mother. I got a lot of things from my mother, which is why I've been in therapy for the past 80 years.

Most Jewish women hate their mothers, but I don't hate mine because she's dead. She said the best thing that ever happened to women was the vote. I said, "Why?" She said, "Because now we can be heard." I said, "I thought you did that by screaming."

My mother was so Jewish: her jewelry was real, but her orgasms were fake.

She yelled at my father so much that when she died, he thought he had gone deaf.

After her funeral, he took his secretary out. When he got home, he said, "It won't work, Lynn Ruth. She wanted ME to do all the talking." This joke will only work with a Jewish audience. Most people do not get that what I am saying is my father never got a chance to say anything. If there is no laughter, I go on to say: *"Poor Daddy. The only thing I ever heard him say was 'Yes dear.'"*-Then they get it.

It is important to NEVER chastise an audience for not laughing. You insult them and they won't laugh at anything you say after that. Besides, it is your job to make them laugh. The only time you can look at someone who isn't laughing and make a crack is if he is German. Then you say, "That was a JOKE!" and the whole room cracks up.

My mother said, "All smart girls get married." Here I stop and ask someone in the front row, *"Did your mother tell you that?"* I get a nod all too often, and I always say, *"I am so sorry."*

But my God, ladies, look at our choices. Present company excepted, of course. There are two kinds of men, actually in Brighton (this is any place known for its gay community), *there are three.*

There's the kind who hate their mother. They smoke Marlboros, don't use condoms, and beat their wives. I married one of those. I paused to let that sink in.

Good comedy contrasts tragedy with laughter,

I can still remember his pitching me across the bed saying, "I can't do it! I can't do it!"

"Can't do what?" I asked.

"Grow a mustache," he said.

I said, "Never mind; I can."

Always the enabler. This is the tagline.

Let me tell you about that marriage. After we got engaged, my mother-in-law took me to a butcher shop and pointed to a two-pound chicken and said, "That's how big he was when he was born."

I said, "Nothing much grew, did it?"

He was very nearsighted and wore thick glasses. When he went to bed he would take them off and say "Where are you?"

I'd say, "If you can find me, you can have me."

And that's why I was a virgin when we divorced.

My second husband was a different kind of guy. Another tag line. *My God, he smelled good! He loved his mother, did my nails and danced in the ballet. You should have seen him in tights. (Didn't do ME any good.)*

On our honeymoon, I caught him with the bellboy. I said, "What are you doing?" He said, "Showing him my pas de deux."

I said, "Why is he crying?"

He said, "Because he wanted a tip, and I gave him the whole thing." This is another one that takes time to absorb. It is important when you KNOW a joke is funny to pause and give the audience a chance. Pacing is one of the most difficult and most important arts to master in delivering your comedy.

He was in love with the doctor. He would say, "I have to go to the doctor today to get my checkup."

I said, "You were there five times today. Why not try an aspirin?"

He said, "No, this guy gives me special enemas."

When we got divorced, the judge said, "Thank God there were no children."

I said, "Had there been children, there would have been a second coming. And God knows there wasn't a first."

The first time I did this joke it got no laughs at all. I thought it just was not strong enough. Still, it fit into the story, so I kept it in, always going very fast into the next section. Then I was in a blue-collar bar in Emeryville where English is usually the second language of the residents. I did the joke and it brought down the house. That was when I realized how important it is to be comfortable with your story. I had been telling this sequence for a good three years, maybe more, and by then my timing had become spot-on because that time in the bar in Emeryville I was living the story. That makes all the difference.

I believed what I was going to say. That is why the joke worked. The first few times I was just reciting it.

With a mother like I had and a husband like that, it is no wonder I got an eating disorder. . That means I have a very strange relationship with food. I read cookbooks as if they are best-sellers while I created gourmet meals (that I wouldn't touch) for my husband. When I see someone eating a pizza, I always think "I wish I had the courage to do THAT." And if I see someone like you licking an ice cream cone... I want to fuck it.

Even now, when I have it under control, I am obsessed with food. But my memory is shot and that is why cooking has become a challenge these days. The first thing do when I wake up in the morning is plan what I will eat all day. The problem is that my memory is so bad that by the time it is 6:00(That is dinner time; all Jews eat at 6:00; anything later than that is snacking) I always forget what I had planned to make.

However, the other day, I decided to make risotto for dinner with a green salad and tea. When I got into the kitchen, I remembered! Here the audience claps. If they do not, I have lost them. That is when I need to change direction...not easy to do but important. However this is the middle of a story so I have to find another lead in to get them on board with me. I often say "That is simple isn't it...tea, salad and rice, Right?" And now they are listening.

I poured water in the teapot to boil for the tea I don't like to use plain water on rice, do you? I always ask a specific woman that question and if she says she uses water, I say, "Well I am not coming to dinner at your house." *I use chicken stock So I put that on low to pour on the rice. I like to add some onions to give it flavor. So, I poured olive oil in a frying pan and put it on low to get it ready for the onions. As I was chopping, my contact lens fell out. I finally found it and I took it into the bathroom to put it in the cleaning solution.*

When I came back, the kitchen was filled with smoke and smelled awful. The frying pan had burned out. I took it to the recycle bin and when I got back into the kitchen, the teapot had boiled out, so I took it to the recycle bin.

Well, I couldn't see very well, but I was very hungry, and I could still see color. So, I decided to make the salad. I was afraid I would chop off my thumb or something, but I was careful. I took out the peppers, mushrooms, celery and started chopping when I heard a loud ring in my ear. The battery in my hearing aid had gone dead.

I pulled it out, but my hands were wet, and it fell on the floor. I bent over to find it when I heard another pop!OMG! The second kettle had just burned out. I took that out to the recycle bin and I thought, "The hell with it. I'll order out."

But I couldn't see the phone number on the fridge, and I wouldn't be able to hear the guy when he answered the phone anyway, but I could still see big shapes. So, I decided to drive to The Seven-Eleven.

The policeman took me to the emergency ward, and they kept me overnight because of the concussion. The lady from Senior Help took me home, found my hearing aid on the kitchen floor, and changed the battery. She took the onion out of the cleaning solution. That is my favorite line in the story. *She found my contact lens and helped me get it back in. She tucked me in bed and said, "Have a good day," and when she left, I looked at the clock. "OMG, it's 6:00 and I have to cook dinner."*

The reason this works is because it is completely ridiculous but not boring. Pace and timing are everything in comedy. I do my stories fairly fast and if you pick them apart, you will see that every third line is a little joke building up to the big finale which is "It was 6:00 and I have to cook dinner.")

They have given me ten minutes up here (or twenty or thirty or 45) *because they think that is all the time I have left. I can hardly blame them. My passport number is 4.*

I've had so many body replacements that when I go through airport security, it sounds like I hit the jackpot in Vegas.

But I love flying now because they explore my sensitive areas. My two husbands couldn't find them.

The thing is you never know if they are going to pull you out of the line. So, I always remember to wear my burqa.

Flying has changed so much since I was young. Gone are the days when you could give your ticket to the attendant, board the plane, throw your rifle in the overhead, roll a joint, sit back and relax.

Now it's all about security. I love the patting down. The last guy who did it looked just like my first boyfriend. When I got in the line, I got so excited I felt a flutter, and I thought I better calm down, or else I would say something awful like "keep going, I left my knickers at home.". So I opened my pill caddy to take out a pill. The security dog jumped up and swallowed the pills and the caddy. Then he dropped dead. Life isn't fair, is it? That dog didn't need Prozac. I did.

Eighty-six sounds so old! When I was a young chick of seventy-nine, I took what I did for granted, but now I am proud of everything I manage to do! For example, this morning, I woke up!

I turned the gas off on the stove. I don't do that every day!

I had sex... with myself. I wanted to be sure my partner was still alive.

When you're my age, your body changes. You lose inches and you also get shorter. I look at one of the guys in the audience. *Sorry, darling*

I have gotten so short I don't need to bend over when I wash the floor, and I don't have to go down to go down.

There are so many jobs now for seniors. I have such great legs that several senior facilities have hired me to open them up all over the country.

I model support hose in Laura Ashley prints, and non-skid nappies for seniors on the run.

And I'm the perfect height to be a fluffer. I often get puzzled looks here, so I say something like "Google it" which gets as big a laugh as the joke.

But then I looked in the mirror and decided I would be better as a fluffer control. If he gets too fluffed, I just give him a grandmotherly look. Down it goes!

I have been around a long time! I did cruise ships! I did the Mayflower. I knew John Smith, but he wanted Pocahontas, and I don't do sex that way.

I was a centerfold for Popular Mechanics.

My hip was featured in Playboy... *in the gadget section.*

I put my kidney on eBay under collectibles and I got a bid from an archaeologist.

He was into dinosaurs...but I'm tighter than that. Another joke that needs a long pause.

Time was, when I wanted fast cash, I sold the jalopy. And now I am the jalopy.

When I do a long set, I intersperse the one-line jokes with little silly stories. This, like the risotto disaster, is one of them. It is important when you do these stories to move around as much as you can and put a lot of expression in your voice.

Erma Bombeck said a clean house is the sign of a wasted life. Anyone who knows me knows I have not wasted one minute of my life. A few years ago, my friend Louise came to visit me and said, "Lynn Ruth, this place is a mess. I know someone who will clean the place for cheap."

I said, "Listen, Louise, why should I pay for something I can do myself? Besides, once you get someone else to do for you, you might as well go into assisted living. Right?"

I felt guilty about the mess I lived in though, so the next morning I put the soap, the cleanser and the rags on the kitchen counter. I looked up and realized a light bulb needed changing. Well, I have gotten really short, remember? So, I got out a chair and put the Webster's Dictionary *and the first three volumes of the* Encyclopedia Britannica *on it so I could reach the bulb. While I was doing this, the dog heard a noise and came charging into the kitchen. He bumped into the chair and I fell into the spray cleaner; the light bulb crashed on the counter and my hip broke the faucet. It gushed water to the ceiling, and all I could think of was, "Oh my God, I can't swim,"*

Well, they let me out of the hospital in three months and other than having to get new dentures ,and replacing my hip I felt much better. I decided to have a private physician replace my hip because my friend Brenda let her health service do it and she went deaf.

I sat down at the desk to pay the bills for this debacle while I was waiting for Louise to bring me my gruel. By the time I paid for the ambulance, the three surgeries, the physical therapy, the walker and pulley, the plumbing remodel, the vet bills and the new encyclopedia, it came thousands. I was writing checks when Lucy came in. She looked at my house and said, "OMG, Lynn Ruth, this place is a fucking mess. I can get someone to clean it for cheap." But I said, "Listen, Louise I don't need someone to clean the house. I need someone to change a light bulb."

Everyone is afraid of ageing. I am here to tell you there is nothing to be afraid of. This has been the best year of my life! Of course, I can't remember any of the others.

I am on my third car this year! I can't remember where I parked the other two.

I know I'm wrinkled. I used to tell everyone these were laugh lines, but then I realized nothing could be THAT funny.

Listen, you can see these things on Google Earth. The reason I tell you that is I want you to know that despite my age, I can use a computer. So, let's try again: You can see these things on Google Earth. The punch line is supposed to be Google Earth, but it never gets as big a laugh as "so I am going to tell you that joke again, and you are going to laugh."

I am so wrinkled, I took my bulldog to the vet, and they gave me the shot. This is the funny line, but it always gets lost because everyone is laughing at hearing a joke twice.

When you are my age, people think you don't matter. The lifeguard pulled me out of the pool, looked at me and said, "You've been in here a LONG time!" Then he threw me back in.

I admit it: My cleavage is so cross-hatched I could play naughts and crosses on it... if I could find the pencil.

People ask me why I wear a bra: I said to keep them from hanging out the bottom of my blouse.

These days I go to Hooters for the memory. But what's worse: My boyfriend goes for the food.

The medical community does some of the dumbest studies. It spends millions of dollars to study things we already know. For example: They did an extensive study on the male condition and they concluded that testosterone is toxic... I figured that one out after the first divorce.

And they discovered that more men commit suicide than women.... which all goes to show they can do SOMETHING right.

The study said a man's penis is three times the size of his thumb. Let's see your thumb! We know they are wrong, don't we, ladies? It is about one-tenth the size he says it is.

Americans have a strange relationship with food. We all want to be skinny but don't want to give up dessert. So, the medical profession stepped up to the plate: They designed a gastric band. They tie it around your stomach, and you aren't hungry. There are side effects though: bloat, gastritis, heart attack... wouldn't it be cheaper to put the band around the refrigerator?

Now that I am older, the medical profession has decided it can make a lot of money on the elderly by inventing procedures that remind us that we are falling apart, and they are not. You are supposed to have a colonoscopy every ten years after you turn fifty. They put a pipe up your ass and then you're on television. I was excited about this because I have been trying to get on TV for years. They clean out your intestine with a drink they have named GoLightly. For most people, this is like swallowing liquid dynamite, but it didn't work on me.

The doctor said, "Don't worry. I have a plan B." Listen, if a doctor ever says he has a plan B, walk out of that office and go to a faith healer.

They gave me pills with fuses and a warning: DO NOT OPEN IN AN ENCLOSED SPACE. I saw the very same pills in the hardware store in the demolition section. I blew out the side of the house and shattered the bay window, but they did the job (and so did I).

At the exam, they sedate you so you're woozy but not asleep. When you do that to a comedian, what does he do? Right. He tells jokes (which I did).

So, the doctor is looking at a screen and laughing and I am thinking. What is he laughing at? My jokes? Or what he sees on the screen? Because if it is what he is seeing, I am in trouble. At the end of the examination, my doctor said, "I want to thank you. I have never had so much fun." I said, "Well, what did you expect? Look at the profession you chose."

The credit crunch has everyone so scared. I am here to reassure you. Do not worry. I lived through so much worse: The Depression... The Dust Bowl. But enough about my sex life.

The truth is if other parts of my body dripped as much as my nose, I would have a much more exciting love life.

The trick to living cheaply is to substitute what you can afford for what you want. When I hanker for hot fudge. I go out with a black guy.

If we want Neapolitan, we go to a casino and hug the dealer.

I love cheese, so when I want something stinky and expensive, I hire a homeless gigolo.

Everyone has guilt issues about the elderly and if you play it right it's worth money. I was having tea at a cafe and when I tried to pay, the waitress said, "That's all right, sweetie. You just enjoy your biscuit. Shall I soak it for you?" I thought, if it works here, maybe it will work at a department store.. Well, it didn't. The judge gave me six months for shoplifting. But I appealed, and he reduced it to life. I always pause here so they can figure that one out. It is another one of those jokes they have to think about and since I KNOW it is good, I wait until they do the math.

Still, I am so happy to be ageing! A lot of my friends didn't. That's why I read the obituaries... for romantic leads. If the survivor is male and can drive, I'm at that viewing. With my credit score, my phone number and a casserole... those guys are always hungry.

I love funerals: the incense, the flowers, the hot prospects. You can get used household items and great clothing if you work it right.

I found a gorgeous guy at Woodlawn Cemetery last week! Well-dressed, his own teeth... He was ninety years old. He drove over to my house in a 1933 Ford. Listen, anything that old is going to have something broken, something missing and something leaking, right? And the car was a mess, too.

So, I Googled my high-school boyfriend. And I found him! We made a date for 7:30 for dinner, and I decided this time I'd wear clothes. Pause here. *He knew me when I was watertight... and didn't need ironing.* And here I stop and point to the floor and say "I didn't do that."

He came over at 7:30 in the morning... I said, "No, we had a date for dinner."

And he said, "I know, but I can't see to drive at night." Welcome to the senior condition.

So, there we were at Subway, because he had a coupon.

He was whispering sweet nothings in my good ear. (That's this one.) I was wiping the applesauce off his bib and we were having a spirited discussion about glucosamine when he said, "Whoops! There goes my hearing aid. You'll have to sign."

I said, "If this is on me, you're not."

At my age, if you don't pay, I don't play.

Now I have a new boyfriend. He's French and Russian, but I'm faster. He's sixty years old so I don't like being seen out with him in public. I don't want to be arrested for pedophilia. He sends me wonderful emails.

I stop here and look at a couple and say, *"Does he send you great emails?"* She will always nod, and I will say, *"Or does he just call and say knickers off, I am on my way home?"*

My guy sends lovely emails. Always try to repeat your set ups a couple times if you can...and do not swallow the punch line. Say it slowly. That is your bread and butter.

He said I reminded him of Mother Theresa. Pause here and look puzzled. *Does Mother Theresa swallow?* This seems like the punch line to my audience, and I often get a shocked gasp because I said such a thing and then uproarious laughter. And then I say the real punch line: *"Not anymore."*

Jokes often take a long time to develop. It has to be fifteen years ago that I thought of the Mother Theresa idea, but I didn't have a very funny punch. I thought "Is Mother Theresa Jewish?" And that was worth a smile but not a laugh. and then one of the men I was doing comedy with came up with "Does Mother Theresa swallow?" I was not sure what that meant, but I knew it got a huge laugh, so I used it. However, when I tried the joke to a conservative audience in Newcastle, it upset half of them that I would say such a thing and the other half didn't know what I was talking about. Jonathan Mayer, one of the finest comedians on the planet, was my MC that night. He waited until what laughs there were died down. Then he took the mike and said, "Not anymore!" And that is the perfect call back. I have used it ever since.

Let's hear it for women. We have come such a long way. Nowadays no one wants a mink coat... except a mink.

We thought a diamond was a girl's best friend. Now it's Botox... or a GPS.

When my husband was angry, I served him a great dinner. You girls serve him papers.

We thought you had to have a man to make a baby. Now all you need is a good sperm bank and a reliable thermometer.

Anything is possible for anyone these days. I have always wanted a baby. With all that stuff frozen, it might just be my time. Long pause here to let that sink in. *But I don't want to go to one of those fertility clinics. All those babies look like the doctor.* Another pause.

And what is this with tattoos? I saw a reptile on that girl's shoulder. In my day you didn't wear a snake, you divorced him.

I saw a teenager with Peter Pan tattooed on the small of her back. What was she thinking? In thirty years, she'll be sitting on him.

But I like to look hot. These days if you want to be cool you have piercings: your nose, your ears, your tongue. I think I am pretty hot, don't you? I wait for applause here. *A GILF?* Pause again to say, "Who said yes."

So, I got myself a nipple ring... I keep my car keys on it so that I won't lose them. I just get in the car, unlace my trainers ... and there they are!

In my old hometown, we had an all-woman city council. It was great! All the restrooms had full-length mirrors, hair dryers, and air fresheners in every stall. But then they all got PMS at the same time and blew up the police department. Which wasn't a BAD thing...but the city went broke... no citations.

I know what you are thinking and yes, you can after eighty... but carefully. It's like the horizontal two-step. You know: one, two and it's over. But it's a lot more relaxing. Guys my age can't see what they're getting and fall asleep before they get it. And they all have replaced hips and arthritic joints. When they really get going, it sounds like a dress rehearsal for STOMP.

The nice thing about dating at my age is you don't have to worry about meeting their parents. One guy told me he wanted me to meet his mother. He came to my door with a shovel.

Men my age have such hubris! One guy said, "Boy wait 'til you see my package!" And it was immense! It had his respirator, insulin and a holster. I said," Where is the gun?" He said, "It backfires." I said, "That's what you get for being a vegetarian."

I can't count the times I used to wake up and the guy was gone. Now when he locks me in his embrace, I kick his walker out of reach, and he is right there in the morning. If he gets too frisky, I just pinch his oxygen tube. That does it.

I tried speed dating, but it doesn't work for the elderly. The first guy got his foot caught in my walker; the second one dropped his teeth in my beer. It isn't for me.

I try to keep up with the times, though. I love to go to raves… I just turn off my hearing aid and put my pacemaker on vibrate.

Old men! They only want one thing! Sleep. And when they give you that look, you know what they're after: Their teeth.

Poor guys. They are such lousy housekeepers. But I always say, "It's not the size of your vacuum cleaner, it's how you use it."

I'm through with old men! But they aren't finished with me. They keep groping me... especially the ones who can't afford guide dogs. Here is another one that used to fall flat but does not anymore. Still when I say it, I always stop and say, *"I really love that joke. The idea of some old man groping me and thinking I am a German Shepherd amuses me. I mean you KNOW what the Germans did to the Jews....* Here, I get a huge laugh even though that sentence does not make sense at all. *So, I am going to tell that again and you are going to laugh.* Again, they laugh at the fact that I insist on repeating it.

I try to end my club sets with this routine because it is reliably funny. *"I do get lonesome now and then, so I decided to try internet dating. How many of you have tried that?* There will be sparse applause and I will say, *"There are a lot of liars in this place!"*

But it is hard to find the right one when you are my age. For example, I cannot go out with someone on Match.com because the oldest man on that site is sixty. I cannot go out with someone who is sixty years old! I will be arrested for pedophilia!

Well, I finally found the perfect website for me. GDate.com (geriatric date...) I didn't know what picture to put up there, though because they all lie. So, I put up the picture of my mother changing my diaper. Of course, I change my own now.

I don't think a site like that should have headshots, do you? No. You want body scans. You want to know: Is the hip his? Do the teeth come out at night? It's a whole different blow job if the teeth come out at night.

One guy called me up and said, "I want to take you to Starbucks."

Starbucks is an exciting date when you are my age. You get caffeine! So, I said "Yes! I would like that."

And he said, "Fine, I'll pick you up at 7:30. How many steps to your front porch?"

I said, "Two."

He said, "Well then, I'll just honk, and you come out."

Well, *I don't know if he got there at 7:30, because at 7:30 I was looking for my hearing aid. I never did find it until I went upstairs to get my teeth, but by that time, the batteries were soaked.*

Not one person in this room understands that joke.

So, I am going to explain that joke with another joke: A man was walking down the street with a suppository in his ear. Someone said, "Did you know you have a suppository in your ear?" and he said, Oh! Now I know what happened to my hearing aid."

Now you know where I put MY hearing aid. In the glass.

I finally did meet that guy! He was the shortest man I have ever seen. He walked with two crutches like a gorilla on a mission. Why you men walk like this when you get to be a certain age is beyond me. It is as if you want to protect something that...doesn't need protection anymore.

Well, there we were at Starbucks and he gave me a twenty and told me to get whatever I wanted. So, I got a cab and went home.

***

None of this has been memorized but it has all been written down. The amazing thing is that if I listen to a tape of these jokes, I realize that I always use the exact same phrases in exactly the same way.

The truth is there is no fast road to success in comedy. I have been very lucky. I have only bombed twice, meaning gotten no laughs at all, but I have had plenty of nights where the laughs were sparse. Thank goodness now that almost never happens to me. But it took sixteen years and I still have a long way to go before I feel totally on top of the art.

That is why I keep at it. I keep thinking, pretty soon I will get there; but the minute I reach one pinnacle there is another looming in front of me and I know I must try for that one.

CHAPTER 11
The Best Accident

When I look back at the different roads my life has taken since that day in 1933 when I entered the world, I realize I have been more than a dozen people in my lifetime. Oh, sure, I've had the same name, but I didn't have the same attitude, the same fears or even the same look. I guess you could say that I am just a different variation of the human being I once was. The core is still there…or is it?

On a fluke, I turned my life around at seventy, an age when society encourages us to slow down and retreat inward. Now I'm an international performer in my eighties! I've never stopped learning, growing, and changing. Why should I? Life improved for me exponentially once I was in my seventh decade of life. There is far too much to do and far too little time to get it all done.

Another important part of my personal growth came with the decision to change countries when I turned eighty. First, I went to Brighton for two years and then a miracle happened, and I was able to move to London (although I still spend lots of time in the US and I pay my taxes there).

When I crossed that ocean, I thought I was just making a new life, but it was so much more than that. I was defying stereotypes, smashing glass walls and forcing people to come face to face with their prejudices…the ones that say the older you are, the less you can do; the ones that say women aren't funny; the ones that say old women aren't the image we want to project. The more I pushed, the more I insisted on being seen, the more I got the laughs no one thought I would get, the more I cracked the wall that still keeps me out of the big time. And that wall IS crumbling, very slowly.

In September 2013, I returned to Pacifica to pack up my belongings, solidify the house sale, and move to England. But before I left the United States and the San Francisco Bay Area for the UK, I had THE most amazing weekend in Sacramento at The Punch line. Paul Mercurio was the headliner and I was very worried that he would object to me the way the comedian had at Cobbs. To my delight and surprise, we got along as if we were old, old friends. Lee Levine was the feature and he was also a nice human being. It was an amazing week and one I will never forget. When I told Paul I was a stripper, he said he didn't believe me so at the finale, when I finished the show, I took off my shirt…I guess you had to be there.

I returned to the UK on April 24, 2013. I believed that this was a good decision for me and for the career I had been building for nine years. I arrived first in London and stayed with Sarah-Louise Young in Stockwell. We went out for dinner at a lovely pub and as always when I am with her, I was filled with optimism and hope. She is as near to an angel as anyone I have ever met. The next day I took the bus to Brighton.

I was busy from the moment I arrived there working on the show I planned to create for Edinburgh after my big win the year before and doing as much comedy as I could manage, mostly in London. The pace I kept up then is pretty much the way I am living my life now, except that now I also fly all over the world, Asia, Europe, Australia and America. However the real beginnings of this began in London and Brighton. Here is the schedule I created once I got to the United Kingdom. I have not slowed down.

The night after I returned to Brighton from San Francisco, I took the train into London to do Inkey Jones' Room. It was the most difficult room I have ever played because it was fuelled with only tourists from a variety of countries.

It was at Kingsway Hall Hotel in Covent Garden, and we do two shows back to back. Inkey has a very particular kind of comedy: he works the audience and has very little original material. I cannot do that. I am far more comfortable if I have tried out my jokes a few times in unpaid gigs before I present them to a paying audience.

When I got to the club, I discovered Inkey had given me two very long sets. My first set that night was so-so, but the second was great and my confidence returned. I was ready for the next evening when I was doing the Komedia's Funny Women show back in Brighton. It was a stellar night, as it always is, and we all went out for a drink after, stayed too late and laughed too much. Saturday night, I did another show at Komedia and at midnight I performed at the Mesmerist Bar walking down the stairs and singing a strip song. Great experience. I got home at two in the morning.

Then Sunday afternoon I did Stories with Tea which is a lovely afternoon event where we sit around a table drinking tea and eating biscuits, while I tell stories from my book THOUGHTS WHILE WALKING THE DOG. I performed two more of those shows that month. At the first one, only three people showed up and one woman was texting the entire time I was speaking. Word of mouth is your best ticket seller and by the third show I packed the house.

The evening after the storytelling show, I hurried over to the Hobgoblin Bar where I told a couple grandma stories that went over well. It was another night where I did not get back to my flat until two a.m.

A good night's sleep was not in the cards because the next day I had an interview with the BBC at noon. We talked about what was special about The Brighton Fringe, a smaller event than Edinburgh that has kept the flavor of a real fringe where people try out new, creative concepts and bring them to the public to see how they fly. It is not as intense (or expensive) as Edinburgh and is much more rewarding. I have to say that this was seven years ago and each year the Brighton Fringe becomes more and more like Edinburgh; ridiculously expensive, and impossible for anyone on a budget to manage more than a couple shows. The advantage of that fringe however is that you do not have to do a whole month of productions there.

That same night I did comedy at the Quadrant in Brighton. I ripped up the room and it made me feel very good. I do not always do well in those rooms. They are always filled with drunks and often my age puts the audience off. However, the booker is always lovely to me and schedules me several times during each festival. On this night, the laughter was marvelous.

The next night I was in Daphna Boram's comedy show in Brighton. It was called *Not Dead Yet,* and featured older comedians (of course I am so old I am actually over the top) with Richard Rycroft who is my favorite, favorite of all the comedians I perform with, ever. That Richard is an ex-policeman and totally disenchanted with law enforcement in England. He said, "When I joined the force, our mission was to make the world a nicer place for nice people, but now it is only to make the world nicer for *us.*" I loved the show and loved the people in it, although I cannot say I was particularly stellar. I hated to admit it , but I was still learning even then ten years into the game.

A few days later, I went into London to do the Funny Women Comedy Show at the Leicester Square theatre. It was raining, and, as usual, I managed to get lost. Still, I got there early, and they would not let me into the theatre. I was sitting in the rain outside one of the hotels across the alley from the theatre and the concierge insisted I come inside, and he gave me a cup of coffee. That is the way it is in London, always. People are lovely and considerate to anyone lost, old, or infirm. (I am often all the above.)

My next gig was in Red Hill to perform at a comedy club there. I not only did well, but I got paid, which I did not expect. It was a glorious evening for me. The next night, I was back in Brighton at *The Latest Bar* to host an Awards Ceremony for performances at The Brighton Fringe. (I won Star of Brighton for *Ageing is Amazing* in 2009.)

I was back at the Kingsway Hotel in London on Sunday. Other comedians hate this place because they advertise that they feature professional comedians. Actually, they pay no one but Inkey, who hosts and organizes it. The rest of the lineup is a bunch of rank amateurs. However, I love doing the show; first, because Inkey is there and I respect his talent; and second because he gives me really long sets in two back-to-back shows.

When I first settled into my eyrie above the fish and chips shop in Brighton I looked around for a place to start my own shows like I did when I lived in Pacifica. The Neighborhood is a lovely pub on James Street in Brighton and the owner was up for a monthly comedy show and my first one was that Wednesday. I was worried that no one would show up, but we had a great crowd and the comedians were wonderful. Ria Lina, who is one of my all-time favorite comedians, came down to do a preview of her Edinburgh show, and Daphna Baram did a short summary of hers. We had a guest comedian that night from Brighton who was amazing, and the entire show was a success. The owner gave me far more money than I deserved which made me very happy as well since usually I am not paid for Brighton performances. The city has way too much talent and too few places to perform, so most gigs there are not reimbursed.

Friday night, I returned to London to perform at Inkey's show again. That gig ends after midnight so that means a garbage dinner on the late train. However, I managed to get home and pack to go to Stockport Saturday to do comedy for Hazel at The Laughing Cows in Manchester. I did two gigs for Hazel. The first was in Stockport and the next night was The Frog and Bucket. Sadly, they were very mediocre, and I felt defeated. Hazel is a lovely human being and I know I disappointed her. The learning process in comedy can be very painful and, if you are an achiever as I am, it is humiliating to travel such a long way and not feel you earned the money you are paid.

But I had no time to brood over my failure, because the very next day it was time to travel to Edinburgh to do the wild marathon of shows I always do when I am there for the month of August.

When I returned to Brighton at the end of that month I had scheduled a performance at Leicester Square Theatre of GET A GRIP, the cabaret I did that year in Edinburgh. Karen Rosie made posters and, because Karen was a genius at promotion, we filled the house.

Two nights later, I did a reprise of *Granny's Gone Wild* at The Grey's, a venue famous for both music and performance in Brighton. Bill came to that show and it was the first time he had seen it since we put it together the year before. He could not see any difference in my final version (the one that won the

TO&ST Award) which all goes to show how selective our perception is. The place was filled and the show a success.

I continued my marathon of gigs in the UK while preparing for yet another cabaret to do the next August in Edinburgh, when the landlord decided to close the building I was living in, in Brighton. He asked me to please leave as soon as I could but assured me that no one would throw me out. I was, after all, eighty-two years old and alone in the world. That same day I got a letter from Ajex House in London telling me that they had some flats for me to see. One wonderful thing led to another and by September, I had moved to London.

Once there, I did *80! A Cabaret* at the Vauxhall Tavern. The place was filled, and I got a standing ovation. I was stunned. The audience kept clapping and shouting and I just scurried off the stage trying to absorb their accolades. Sarah Bodalbhai played the piano and she was amazing. Thanks to her, I didn't mess up the songs. I had done the same show right before I left for Edinburgh the previous August, and I made a total mess of it. I could see all the people looking at one another then and saying, "This is her last performance… she won't be able to continue like this much longer." The Vauxhall success re-kindled my confidence in the show itself and my ability to perform it. It has become a staple of my repertoire although I change the title every year. It is now called *"86! A Cabaret!"*

From the moment I moved to London, I was on the fabulous journey I am on right now. I started touring the continent—Berlin, Amsterdam, Barcelona and Prague—and then expanded to Manila, Bangkok, Cambodia, Vietnam, Singapore, Melbourne and more... I hope lots more.

One of the things I have not accomplished is to appear on commercial television. Although I had my own programs on Pacifica's Public Access Channel 26 for almost fifteen years, I never have been featured on a talk show on a major channel or managed to get into a sit com. It is only when I look back over the last sixteen years, that I realize how many times I have been featured on major networks throughout the world.

In 2008 after I had been doing comedy for 3 years and had just begun incorporating burlesque into my routine, I got a message in my computer inbox saying, DO YOU HAVE TALENT?

Well of course I did! I answered immediately saying I was the Stripping Granny. Within an hour, I got an email back inviting me to try out for American's Got Talent. I had never heard of the program because I do not have a television set, so I had no idea that there was a monetary award or that the program was national. However, the tryout was in Los Angeles on a weekend when I had intended to go to Ashland, Oregon to see some plays. I called Michelle White, the woman who was going to travel with me, and said, "How would you like to go to Los Angeles instead of Ashland?"

"I would love that," she said.

And the next thing I knew, I was in the midst of one of the most exciting weekends of my life. The judges that year were David Hasselhoff, Sharon Osbourne and Peers Morgan. The host was Jerry Springer. He was backstage when I did my audition and when I got off stage, he said, "Very intelligent set."

I smiled and patted his shoulder. "Thank you, darling," I said.

I had no idea who he was.

By the end of the tryout period, I had been accepted to the next stage of the contest. The young man who was registering me looked at my original application and said, "Why didn't you take off your clothes for the audition?"

"Because you only give us 90 seconds to perform," I said. "I cannot take my clothes off that fast."

"If you found the right person, you could," he said.

"No," I said, "He would take them off for me."

Nonetheless, I was scheduled for the second stage of the elimination in Los Angeles, where I got to know The Kinsey Sicks. They are an outrageous male Jewish Quartet cross-dressed as adorable women, who sing songs like "Don't be Happy. Worry." I met them at my original audition when they were dressed as women and I loved them. When we had our second tryout in LA, I was on the bus with them, dressed as men and I had no idea who they were. I have since seen them perform in Edinburgh. I still cannot believe that I got through that audition and went to Las Vegas and they did not. They are beyond talented. They are legends.

That first night in Las Vegas, there was another elimination and I was sure I would be sent home, but I was not. I enjoyed three nights in a beautiful hotel there with a buffet to die for and the heady experience of meeting one marvelously interesting person after another. One of the men who imitated Frank Sinatra was so into being his character that he wore blue tinted contact lenses. Neil Boyd, the opera singer who won, had failed the year before and he told me that the producers had encouraged him to try out again. He was confident he would win, and of course he did. Every night while we waited to do our sets for the judges, we all gathered in a large waiting area and one of the try-outs played the piano, while we all sang and did circle dances. The camaraderie was special and we all rooted for one another. I felt no sense of competition; just a lot of great people together having fun.

I managed to last until Wednesday of that week. I was one of four people trying out for comedy: a young man from Chicago who could not tell a joke to save his life, Tanya Lee Davis, a little person with a filthy mouth, an impersonator named Matthew and I. At that session, the boy from Chicago and I were eliminated. As I walked back to my hotel room, disappointed and defeated, Matthew (who was the final winner of the four) took my hand to comfort me and said, "The dwarf got the sympathy vote."

"Give me a few more years," I said, "And I will take her on."

Tanya Lee is 3'6" tall. At the time we were together in America's Got Talent, I was 5'2-1/2". Twelve years later, I am now 4'10". I am on my way.

I tried again for that competition the next year, but did not get accepted. It was then that I realized how these reality talent shows are created. We were all trying out for a television show. It had nothing to do with talent. The producers are trying to create a series of excellent shows and, after the first elimination, they decide whom they will feature to win and to lose. For example, when I tried out, there was a woman who floated around the stage singing "I am scattering fairy dust on you" who was a loser, but she appeared on one of the final programs. I did not. Evidently, I was not a colorful enough loser.

Being part of the auditions for America's Got Talent was one of those experiences where it made no real difference if you won or lost. The producers were very caring and kind to all the hopefuls who tried out for that program. We were treated with great respect and, once accepted into the final tryouts, all our expenses were covered. I kept in touch with many of the people who where in those try-outs for years afterwards. Tanya Lee is a special friend of mine still and to my delight, we have performed in several festivals together. She moved to London a few years ago, where she is nationally well known. However, the current lockdown, because of the Covid-19 Pandemic, has eliminated all her work and she is planning to return to the states.

In 2011, a scout from Britain's Got Talent saw me at Sweet Venues in Edinburgh during the August festival and asked if I would like to try out for that program. I remember saying, "Don't you have any British comedians to go on your show?"

She said, "We do; but none are your age."

I had been scheduled to perform at The Stand Comedy Club in Glasgow the weekend that Britain's Got Talent had scheduled their Edinburgh tryouts. It was as if fate wanted me to go to that event, and so I accepted.

I loved that Sunday in Edinburgh. The crew filmed me coming in on a bus and then they filmed me in a variety of situations. You can actually see my tryout on line on Britain's Got More Talent. This was another one of those never to be forgotten experiences. I remember that the tryouts started early in the morning and went far into the night. When I finally got on stage, Anthony McPartlin, part of the duo Ant & Dec ushered me on the stage. He called me Ruth and I called him Antan because I thought his name was Antan Deck. I did nto know he was part of a team. He said, "My name is Anthony," and I said, "I guess we are both wrong, because my name is Lynn."

I was one of the last to tryout and be accepted. I was alone this time; no one was there to support me. As I walked down North Bridge, heady with my victory, I stopped a Pizza Express just as they were closing. I walked into the restaurant and said, "I have not eaten all day. I just got accepted at Britain's Got Talent. May I come in?"

And they not only served me, they kept me company while I told them all about the try-outs.

The next elimination was in London and the organizers paid for my trip across the ocean from California. They put us up at The Palace Hotel on the Strand. When I got to the try-out session, I saw a group of elderly singers called The Zimmers. They were in a waiting area filled with oxygen tanks, Zimmer frames, crutches and wheel chairs. As soon as I saw them, I knew I would not advance. The scout had told me it was my age that interested the judges and now that they had British people even older than I, I was no longer a unique contestant. That night, after I had been told that I did not qualify, I called Richard Daniels who had seen me through so many shows with tiny audiences or none at all; and so many times when I had almost made it but not quite. I said to him, "I am so tired of losing all the time."

And he said," You didn't lose. You were in the top 100 people accepted to that show…" and that was when I understood that just being part of such an interesting, and exciting project was an achievement in itself.

As I toured other countries, I managed to be on many TV news programs, such as ABC in Melbourne, Channel News Asia in Singapore and, here in London, The Women's Hour and the BBC. Channel 5 filmed one of my shows as part of their Party Pensioners series, as well.

The reality series that actually made me feel famous, however, was my appearance in 2016 on Channel 4's First Date series. The producers fixed me up with another author, John Banfield, who was just a few years younger than I. I was 82 at the time. He was a lovely man and a true gentleman. Sadly, the truth is that my mind is my erogenous zone and John did not connect with me on any kind of intellectual level. That is why there was no chemistry between us. The audience who saw that show loved it because I fueled their hope that romance can happen at any age. I was stopped innumerable times (once on an escalator in Marks & Spencer's) and asked if I was the one they had seen on First Date. It was a delightful experience and I was thrilled to be part of the program; but it reinforced my belief that even though everyone wants to believe in instant love at first sight, it doesn't happen that way in real life, any more than instant success happens on the comedy stage. Those wonderful achievements all take time.

I waited a few years before I had the courage to return to the scene of my comedy beginnings. I had worked very hard to become a name in San Francisco and I had failed. However, I did return to the Bay Area late August 2018 almost five years after I left the place. I had scheduled several shows there and in every one I got the standing ovations and accolades I never received while I was living there. I know I have come a long way, and those performances proved it to me. Still, even now. I have a very long way to go.

The weekend of March 13, 2020 the British government recommended that we self- isolate and those over 70 stay in their homes. I had several gigs to do, including one at The Vaults in London where I was underground with hundreds of people crowded together. No one there seemed to be aware that we were in the midst of a pandemic. I can remember one of the other performers saying, "We probably all have gotten it; we just do not know it."

And she was right. By that Sunday, I was aware that I was having trouble breathing and was unusually tired. I lost my sense of taste and smell and my digestion went awry. The next weekend the government made lockdown a rule and everyone stopped taking public transportation and going into shops. All the performances I had a scheduled were cancelled, including those in Edinburgh, London, Amsterdam, Berlin, Ghent, Dublin, Melbourne, and Helsinki. I was mildly ill for the next two weeks and then at the end of March I regained my energy and my zest for the new routines imposed on us. It was not a difficult thing for me to do.

Still, suddenly, and without any warning, I was forced back into the same routine I lived for almost fifteen years while I was recuperating from my mysterious illness in 1966. Once again, I was alone, writing, painting and walking. Of course, there is a huge difference between that life when I was an emaciated, ill human being to this one, where I am healthy, happy and still developing a career. The obvious difference is that I have no dogs and cats to walk and keep me company. I am a stronger, happier more confident person now.

I have been doing several comedy shows on-line and adjusting the "set up, punch, laugh" technique I have been using into a new kind of performance with no visible audience response. It is a new challenge, but I have faced many challenges before and overcome just as many set-backs. I see the international reaction to the Corona-19 Pandemic as part of the huge sea-change we are experiencing throughout the world. Predominantly conservative governments are exerting more and more control over our lives and fostering a growing rebellion against that control. This world is unrecognizable from the one I once knew; and that is not a bad thing. I see positive change coming. I see more concern and action to alleviate global warming, to give us all an even playing field and provide each of us with basic needs like health care, housing and food. I envision a world where every human being will have ample resources to build original and fulfilling lives.

And I see a transformation in the entertainment world that was been my life for sixteen years. More people will want to see shows on their computer and television screens; large mass gatherings will diminish or disappear. We, as human beings, need to resist clinging to our old values and expectations. Progress always involves change. For some, change is terrifying. For me, it is exciting.

I am ready for it.

I am certainly not finished. Not by a long shot. Every day, I add a little more to the mix. *That* is the payoff ageing brings. And that's why it is so unbelievably, delightfully and surprisingly amazing.

EPILOGUE
None of This Should Have Happened

People never see how far they have progressed from their beginnings, while they are living their lives. It is only when you look back that you realize what the path you have taken has cost you and the rewards it has given you.

I've learned that you have to take responsibility for your own life. You have to accept who you are. I used to be terribly upset when anyone disapproved of me, and heartbroken if I hurt another person's feelings. Now, I realize I am not perfect. I will never know everything there is to know. I have a million flaws, and I will very often put my foot in my mouth or do something that is shoddy and shameful. It is never deliberate, but it is the human being I have created. And I am proud of that human being. She is a fighter, and she has compassion for others.

I know now that you can't blame the town you are in if things do not go your way, or your parents for not loving you enough because why should they? They are human beings with their own set of values, and all they do is give you the raw materials to make your own life. They don't have to applaud the result. I was always ashamed that I had never found a husband, never had children, and always lived far below the poverty line even though I was super educated. Then I read a book about what really matters in life, and the author wrote, *you are as perfect as you can be today. If someone objects to you, it is their problem.* And I thought, "Yes! I am as good as I can be today, and tomorrow I will be even better. Why am I so ashamed of who I am?"

I realized then that what others thought of me had nothing to do with my value as a human being. The reason I have never found anyone to love exclusively is that I have not truly loved myself. That is the project I needed to work on first.

Once I started comedy, I began to like the person I am. I started dressing with a bit more flair and because you cannot go on stage and remember all your lines if you are starving, the vestiges of that eating disorder I struggled with for forty years finally vanished.

I realized that when you start a new career, you must play the game. Just because I was seventy instead of twenty-five, I didn't deserve special consideration or a leg up in my climb to the top. I have been doing this now for sixteen years and loving every minute. I have railed against the patronizing attitudes, the unsaid blocks that keep me from headlining in major comedy clubs. I finally realized that what really matters is doing my job, and my job is making people laugh. I do that, and my audiences are wildly diverse.

The side effect of loving what I am doing is that I love the rest of my life, too. I have finally figured out what happiness is, and I have it. I am enjoying who I am and where I am going. I have many, many goals to reach, and I am not nearly where I want to be. Not yet.

That zest for what I do and where I am is what I call happiness. When bad things happen, and they often do, they do not shake my sense of well-being. In the years since I started this beautiful career, I have lost my house, I have lost the job I left a country to take, I have broken both my wrist and my heel, and I have overcome bladder cancer. None of that shook my self-confidence or my belief in a building a vigorous, compelling, and challenging future.

So now I am a part of the international comedy circuit. People look at me and think "Why isn't she in a home, knitting and playing bingo?" Who would believe it all began on a comedy stage in San Francisco when I was seventy years old? I told a joke, and the crowd *went wild*. And presto, I had a new career.

I'm eighty-six years old and officially entering *old, old age*. For those of you that will be lucky enough to make it this far, I am your future. I sing, I dance, I write *and* I even strip…….. sort of. But mainly I tell jokes, funny ones. In fact, I think I am the oldest working stand-up comedienne in the world! Anyone older than I am cannot stand up. In 2019 alone I've played everywhere from Hanoi to Harrogate and I kill *every single time*!

Although I am sixteen years into my career, I'm still working to make it *big*. I see people a quarter of my age playing to arenas while I'm still trying to break through endless glass ceilings. I'm not dead yet! I still have plans. Big ones.

Time is not on my side. Still, we're all living longer, and even though the older I get, the more invisible I become, I am determined to be seen. Life for me did not end at sixty-five. Not even close. I'm beating the path everyone can follow if they dare.

What are *you* going to do when *you* get older? Be like me? Refuse to be ignored? I will not to take "no" for an answer, and I cannot imagine letting myself lie down and fade away. I am walking, talking proof that you can still make it if you try hard enough at any age! I want to be up there with the big boys! And if I can do it, so can anyone. I believe in the impossible. It happened for me and it can happen for you.

I'm Lynn Ruth Miller, and I'm here to fuck up every misconception you've ever had about growing older.

Laughing and growing older. Photo by Nader Shabahangi

Old and Young Comedy in Leicester, UK.

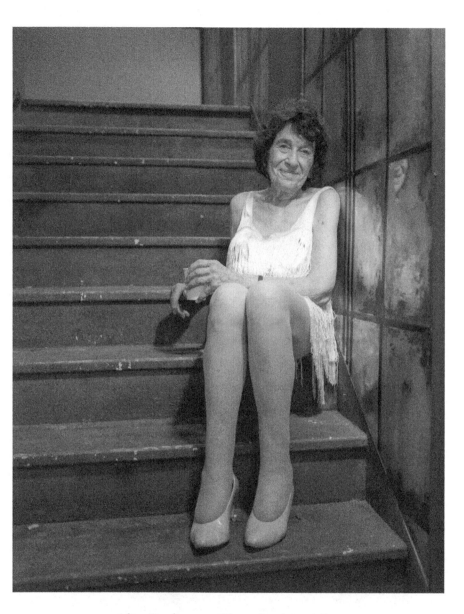

After Burlesque. Photo by Angus Stewart

*A group of men recognised me while I was on my way to a gig
and gave me this fan because they said that is what I am.*

Comedy for Charity, Wimbledon, UK.

I finally made the photo exhibition of notables in the Brighton Station.

My first poster for Singapore.

Performing at the Comedy Masala, Singapore.

Performing at Stand Up NY.

Here I am at my last performance before the pandemic lockdown in March 2020, at The Vaults in London doing burlesque. Photo by Angus Stewart

Made in the USA
Monee, IL
18 August 2020

38760545R00164